blue
rider
press

MY YEAR OF
RUNNING DANGEROUSLY

MY YEAR OF
RUNNING
DANGEROUSLY

A Dad, a Daughter, and a Ridiculous Plan

TOM FOREMAN

BLUE RIDER PRESS *New York*

blue
rider
press

An imprint of Penguin Random House LLC
375 Hudson Street
New York, New York 10014

Library of Congress Cataloging-in-Publication Data

Foreman, Tom.
My year of running dangerously : a dad, a daughter, and a ridiculous plan / Tom Foreman.
p.   cm.
ISBN 978-0-399-17547-3
1. Foreman, Tom.   2. Foreman, Tom—Family.   3. Marathon running—United
States.   4. Fathers and daughters—United States.   5. Marathon running—Psychological
aspects.   6. Aging—Psychological aspects.   7. Long-distance runners—United States—
Biography.   8. Middle-aged men—United States—Biography.   9. Journalists—United
States—Biography.   I. Title.
GV1065.2.F67   2015   2015017237
796.42092—dc23
[B]

Printed in the United States of America
10 9 8 7 6 5 4 3 2 1

BOOK DESIGN BY NICOLE LAROCHE

*Penguin is committed to publishing works of quality and integrity.
In that spirit, we are proud to offer this book to our readers; however,
the story, the experiences, and the words are the author's alone.*

*The names of some runners in this book have been invented because conversations
with them occurred in the course of races and their actual identities are lost in the
limited brain cells of the author.*

For Linda, Ronnie, and Ali—the Foreman Family Running Club

MY YEAR OF
RUNNING DANGEROUSLY

PROLOGUE

As I charge over the hilltop, the trail is a muddy chute flanked by scrub and snow. Powering down the middle with quick strides, I windmill my arms for balance. I head for the flat, where I'll hit dry earth and blast away. Fifty steps left. Twenty. Ten. Calamity.

My left foot shoots sideways. I grab for a branch, miss, and keep spinning with the grace of a hog tossed from a train. The back of my head slams into a tree trunk, and I go down. My vision racks to zero, then screams back into focus. My ears ring and my shoulder goes numb. Cold mud is plastered up one side of my body, and something hot is running down my neck. I press a white glove against my skull and pull it back red.

I have three choices. Remain seated on this remote trail waiting for someone to come along, which might take thirty minutes or three hours. Cut through the woods to the nearest road, and accept that if I go down in transit, I won't be found until next spring. Probably by German tourists. *"Was für ein Tier war das?"* ("What kind of animal was that?") Or . . .

I stagger up, jam my hand against the wound, and keep running. Forty-five minutes later, I burst into my home in suburban

Washington, D.C., in a shower of snow, ice, and mud. My wife, Linda, leads me to the bathroom, checks my pupils for a concussion, and begins washing away the gore. My gloves sit on the sink like evidence in a murder trial.

"You don't need stitches," she says, slathering on antibiotic cream and pushing my hair back into place.

I look at her in the mirror and grin. "Thanks, Dr. Grey."

She answers with a word. "Idiot."

ONE

My descent into the madness of ultrarunning began with a Thanksgiving conversation. The dishes had long been cleared, we'd watched some TV, and I had returned to the kitchen when my eighteen-year-old daughter, Ronnie, asked that question every father dreads.

"How would you feel about running a marathon with me?"

My heart jumped. My pulse raced. A bite of leftover stuffing fell from my fork. As a veteran journalist who has been to war zones, riots, and natural disasters, who has covered serial killers, slipped away from knife-wielding lunatics, and ducked beneath gunfire, I never imagined I would face the most frightening moment of my life in this fashion. And yet there I was, staring into her big blue eyes, wondering how I could escape.

I'd been a marathoner back in my twenties, but now I was knocking—make that pounding—on the door of fifty-one. My knees made strange sounds when I climbed out of bed. You could play "Foggy Mountain Breakdown" on the muscles in my lower back. I had the flexibility of a stepladder, and my weakness for cinnamon rolls had convinced me that covering any sizable number of miles would forevermore involve a combustion engine or a plane ticket.

I squeezed into a sweatshirt and jogged down the road now and then, and I looked fit, but I could feel the toll of too many years of business travel, late nights of work, and bad mealtime choices.

"More fried shrimp, sir?"

"Absolutely! And can I get some extra tartar sauce?"

I remembered two things about marathoning: Training took a lot of time, and I never trained enough. Consequently, my races were exercises in absurdity. I'd start out fast, fall apart in the middle, and by the end be hobbling like some newly discovered Dickens character named Chuffy Dimblewit.

By contrast, Ronnie was young and strong and had embraced the keys to lifelong health: good eating habits, a reasonable amount of sleep, and a work-play balance that allowed her to excel. Her muscles rippled with the power and grace that teenagers take for granted. I wasn't sure what had possessed Ronnie to propose such an idea, and I triangulated a fast end to the conversation.

"You know, honey, training for such a long race can be very hard."

She looked at me and said nothing.

"And remember, it is your first year in college. What are you studying? Juggling?"

"Aerospace engineering."

"That sounds like a lot of work. Physically, this would be very tough. I'd hate to see you get hurt. You know some women wind up sterile!"

Nothing. I sighed the way a man might when the judge asks if he understands the charges.

"Okay. When do we start?"

I took cold comfort from the knowledge that over several decades the image of marathoners has morphed from that of insane masochists who spend far too much time discussing black toenails to borderline normal. If you tell people you have completed a marathon, they are now more likely to greet you with "Congratulations!" than "Dear God, why?" Certainly, for this metamorphosis to have happened, someone must have found an easier way to cover such a daunting distance.

The numbers suggest so. Each year about a half-million Americans tie on their shoes, rub Vaseline into their crotches, and complete one of more than 1,100 of these annual asphalt expeditions.

Many will tell you that it is one of the best experiences of their lives, but it doesn't come easy. In addition to the routine discomforts of profuse sweating, lung-splitting hypoxia, and muscle aches better associated with prisoners in Russian gulags, long-distance runners risk many other maladies: blisters, pulled muscles, heatstroke, hypothermia, sunburn, frostbite, shin splints, scrapes, bruises, dehydration, chafing, joint pain, collapsed arches, kidney failure, stress fractures, hip dislocations, chest pains, back spasms, athlete's foot, crotch rot, and something called iliotibial band syndrome.

Usually, these problems are passing. Sometimes they are permanent.

Either way, most of these runners are content to say that they ran that gauntlet once and join the less than 1 percent of

Americans who can make that boast. They will wear their commemorative T-shirt to every family event, retell the terrors of the road to much hilarity, and slap a 26.2 sticker on the back of their cars to tell the world, "Been there. Run that." If they're faster than Oprah, so much the better. The Queen of Daytime Talk ran D.C.'s Marine Corps Marathon in 1994 in 4:29:15, which is about average. (I assume she did not carry a wallet, because a billion dollars, even in large bills, can slow you down.) If this were a scientific experiment, these recreational runners would be considered the control group because they are more or less normal.

A degree above that crowd are runners who take part in several marathons, usually over several years, and want to get faster. They are seekers of the elusive personal record, or PR. This is not to be confused with being PO'd, which is what happens when they invest several months in training, find a flat course on a cool day, and somehow finish 12 minutes slower than they did last time. These runners are likely to have a sweaty photo of themselves as their Facebook profile pic, to follow *Runner's World* on Twitter, and to have cached a series of notes in their smartphones about training, hydration, and recovery foods. They belong to local running clubs, and they enthusiastically greet every call for fund-raising at the PTA with "Let's hold a fun run!" They drape perspiration-soaked shorts and socks over the edge of the tub, they like to refer to their shirts as singlets, they are forever insisting that they have worn out perfectly good pairs of shoes and that they're "nursing a pulled quad," especially when the dog needs walking. At my best, I was once part of this moderately competitive group.

Then there are the running animals. If there really is a runner's high, these are the addicts. They get twitchy if their training drops below 50 miles a week. They inhale the fumes of moldy, fungus-filled shoes the way wine connoisseurs sniff merlots. They do everything the previous groups do, plus they have ten years' worth of old running magazines in a closet because one of them (they're not sure which one) has "an awesome description of the Ethiopian team's diet!" Their homes and offices are plastered with inspirational running posters that say things like "Dying is easy. Overpronating is hard." Their kitchens are mad scientist labs of protein powders, performance gels, and vitamins. Their default outfit, winter and summer, is running gear in all its permutations. For formal events, they'll pull on jeans, but announce, "Hey, I'm wearing my running shoes. I don't care what you say, Deana." They are largely solitary and can be approached for conversation only when the subject is running, and even then they'll recoil from anyone who does not automatically genuflect at the name Kip Kiprotich.

And they run rapidly enough to win or at least place in the top ten of any given race. They are focused, fast, and not to be trifled with. I once saw a casual runner come between a competitive runner and an energy bar and lose a hand. Not really, but you get my point.

The kindest souls in all these running groups will tell you the same thing if you decide to take up marathoning at my age. See a doctor first. Get a checkup. Make sure that you don't wind up gasping for breath, clutching your sternum, and meeting Saint Peter with a number pinned to your chest. *"Welcome, my son! I'm guessing you were in the Chicago Marathon?"*

Still, even though I'd heard this sage advice all my life, I made an immediate, conscious, and inexplicable decision in the face of my daughter's surprise request. I would not get a physical, I would not stretch, and I would not even buy new shoes.

I would just run.

TWO

Ronnie's target, now unexpectedly mine, was the Publix Georgia Marathon, which started about a mile from her dorm at the famed Georgia Institute of Technology in Atlanta. The race was sixteen weeks away, so the following morning, as Linda toasted bagels, Ronnie and I were at the kitchen island, leaning over a laptop, sorting through a bewildering collection of training schedules.

"Here's one that promises to help us lose weight," Ronnie said.

"Is that what we're after?" I asked.

"Not really. But it wouldn't hurt."

"Look at this one," I said. "'From Zero to Marathon in Six Months.' What do you think?"

"I think we only have four months."

"I was a drama major. Math was not my strong suit."

"Still."

"How about this: 'Marathon Boot Camp!'"

"I don't like the sound of that," Ronnie said. "Mom, what do you think?"

"I'm agnostic on this," Linda said, pulling out some plates. "Where is your little sister?"

"Still asleep," Ronnie said. She turned back to the computer, and her face brightened. "Hey, look here!"

She was pointing to a tidy grid that had popped up on a website, covered with days and distances. It fit our schedule perfectly. It started with short jogs, stepped up to middle-distance trots, and ended with some impressively long runs before the race. To my relief, it also included plenty of days for resting.

"I think we have a winner," I said.

"Hmm. Maybe not. Seems like a lot of days of not running." Ronnie scowled as if she suspected this was some sort of senior citizen fitness plan. "Are you sure this will get us ready?"

"It'll work just fine, Uta," I said.

"Uta?"

"Uta Pippig. She was a great female marathoner. Won Boston three times."

"Whatever. It still seems like a lot of time off."

"Did I misunderstand something yesterday? Didn't you say you wanted me to help you train for this?"

"Yes," she said, letting the *s* hiss like the air from a tire.

"That makes me sort of like a coach."

"Only sort of."

"It's a long process getting ready for this kind of race, and it will go better if you trust me. Anyway, you will need those rest days." God knows *I* will, I thought.

She frowned again and went back to studying the chart as we ate.

I understood. When I was eighteen, I assumed the only way

to prepare for such a thing was to run every day as far as possible. Taking it easy was for losers. That's probably why my plans seldom worked. Even young legs need recovery time.

"Okay," she said after another minute, jumping up to carry her plate to the sink, "so how do we start?"

I looked at Linda, who chewed a piece of bagel with a bemused smile.

"Let's gear up," I said, "and we'll give it a go."

Ronnie disappeared upstairs for five minutes and returned in a pair of cute black running shorts, a yellow Georgia Tech long-sleeve top, and a pair of bright purple shoes. Her leg muscles twitched as she bounced into the room. She already looked like a runner.

I plunged into the back of my closet and dug out some ratty basketball shorts, a wrinkled T-shirt with a picture of the Unabomber, a Troy State sweatshirt in tribute to my own alma mater, and a decrepit pair of Nikes that were faintly green from mowing the lawn. I looked like someone on a prison work-release program. It was good enough. As committed as I was trying to be, this first run was a test of whether either of us would truly be up to this, and I saw no reason to fret about fashion yet.

"Do we need a watch?" Ronnie asked as we stepped onto the road in front of the house, with the sun shining through the chilly air.

"Not yet. We're going to start easy."

"How easy?"

"So easy that our time doesn't matter. So easy that I won't regret it later, I hope."

Like the start of the proverbial journey of a thousand miles, our run began with one step. Then another. We cleared a block, turned along a major boulevard, dropped down to a nearby park, and came out into another neighborhood, and just like that, we were running. Ronnie was chatty and enthusiastic. "This is fun!" she said as we wound along.

I was not so sure. My legs felt rubbery and uncoordinated. The smooth interplay of energy, balance, and movement that I had known long ago was absent. I had to consciously think about each stride, as if I were on stilts. Ronnie was prattling about fences, dogs, houses, and cars. She was pointing out birds in trees and cats in windows. I was thinking, "left, right, left right." My feet slapped the road. A bagpiper falling down stairs would have made less of a wheezing sound. Ronnie asked about my previous marathons, how I was feeling, whether we were running too fast or too slow, and where, precisely, one might find the hamstring.

"Not sure," I gasped. "Somewhere on the back of your leg, I think." To be honest, every time in my life I'd heard that term it had conjured images of meats hanging over deli counters, which pretty well described my ass at the moment.

She was full of questions like "How many Priuses do you think are in this neighborhood, and is that the right plural? Seems like it should be Prii."

And "Hey, did you hear who's going to be in the new *Spider-Man* movie?"

And "Do you like your shoes? That faint green looks kind of cool. How'd you do that?"

I didn't have many answers, but it did not matter.

"I've heard if you can carry on a conversation while running, that's the right pace," she said. "Do you think that's true?"

"Maybe. But sometimes you shouldn't talk at all," I said. "Like maybe now."

Her questions kept flying, and gradually I realized they were helping. I have read that a lot of athletes rely on this sort of dissociative thinking to get past tough spells in training. It works like this: If you can think about the Battle of Waterloo, toaster ovens, or Angelina's tattoos instead of your pending heart attack, you may be able to stretch out your performance— kind of the way Wile E. Coyote can keep running for a while after he's gone off the cliff as long as he doesn't look down.

Under her steady barrage, I lost track of the turns, the inclines, the puffing and panting, my burning lungs, and my dying legs. I forgot about the struggle of running. Three miles after we started, we came back to our house. I was drenched in perspiration, but my outlook had brightened. The pain was real, but so was the possibility that perhaps I could tackle this thing and get, if not good, at least better.

"This is going to be great!" I told Linda after I showered. "Ronnie and I are each going to use the same training plan, and we'll text every day about how our runs went. By the way, do you mind if I stick a schedule on the refrigerator? I really think this will work out well."

She smiled with the boundless patience that had sustained her through a quarter century of marriage to an unnaturally enthusiastic man. "I'm sure it will," she said.

She had reason to be skeptical. When we'd met in Alabama many years earlier, I was in my twenties and more or less playing at running. I would cover some impressively long distances at times, but I was wildly inconsistent. One day I would barely go a half mile; the next I would slam out ten, twelve, or fifteen.

Following the crazy logic of lovesick young men, I would plan my long runs to take me down a road where I thought Linda might be driving. In my mind, this would lead to a romantic encounter with me in the starring role.

"What are you doing way out here?" Linda said, pulling to the shoulder, tossing her honey-blond hair. Her blue eyes swept over Tom's glistening skin and smooth muscles. His thighs bulged. His abs rippled.

"Oh, just out for a little fifteen-mile jaunt," Tom said, grinning. "Want to join me?"

She bit her lip and suppressed a lusty smile

It did not work out that way. Most of the time I ran up and down the same stretch of road so often, hoping to see her, that the neighbors were ready to call the cops. Once, when I had been running there so long that I was prepared to collapse from exhaustion, I spotted her car, only to watch her breeze past while fiddling with the radio, oblivious to my presence. And on the rare times we met, she seemed less aroused than repulsed.

"Oh my, you are one sweaty guy."

Nonetheless, in between movies and dinners I was always dropping lines about how I needed to "train" or "keep up with the entries in my running log." In truth, my training was always catch-as-catch-can, and although I faithfully purchased a shiny red runner's log with a spiral binding each December, by the end of January it would be gathering dust on my night-stand beneath a pile of *Rolling Stone*s, cassette tapes, and books of card tricks.

On one occasion, she agreed to ride her bicycle alongside as I ran twenty miles on back roads in the dead of summer. She was from New Jersey, had moved to Montgomery for work, and would much later admit that she'd assumed I'd suffered from some sort of congenital defect to even attempt such a feat under the blazing Dixie sun. But she came along, and sure enough, about ten miles out I crashed. I had stopped sweating as I became intensely dehydrated. My knees, my legs, and my back buckled. I barely had the strength to walk, let alone run.

"What can I do?" she asked, pedaling to a stop and glancing up and down the endless asphalt between the cotton fields. She looked as cool as if she had been dicing cucumbers and sipping lemonade. "We don't seem to be near anything." In retrospect, I assume she meant we were nowhere near a state home that would take a new patient on a moment's notice.

"I don't know," I groaned. "Maybe you can ride your bike back into town and get your car?"

We hadn't been dating that long, so it was an ambitious request. I couldn't have blamed her if she'd made it home, called the next guy on her long list of suitors, and written me off as lost in the wilderness and devoured by possums—a tale that wouldn't be immediately discounted in that neck of the woods. But she did as I asked. I was staggering down the highway, seeing visions of Jesus in the mirages, when her little white Nissan came streaking to the rescue, complete with air-conditioning and a cold bottle of water she'd brought to revive me.

So, with this new endeavor looming large, I wasn't surprised to sense a mix of encouragement and caution, and I wondered what was on her mind. By late afternoon, I knew.

Ronnie was on an airplane back to Georgia Tech, and I was building a fire in the family room. Our sheltie, Nola, was snoozing nearby. The buzz of having our family of four together for the holiday was fading, taking with it the infectious enthusiasm for what I was already calling "the big run." More important, the aftereffects of the morning were arriving: tightness along the backs of my legs, twinges in my knees. Our high school daughter, Ali, a human fountain of sarcasm, strolled in and flopped on the sofa. Although she has played her share of soccer, is a natural runner, and has a competitive streak a mile wide, she also has an easygoing manner that suggests no physical contest is worth much strain. She sipped a can of diet soda and eyeballed me while I lit some newspaper beneath the logs. As I stood, my left Achilles tendon zinged as if plugged into a wall outlet. I sucked in and winced.

"So, Dad," she said, smirking. "How's the training going?"

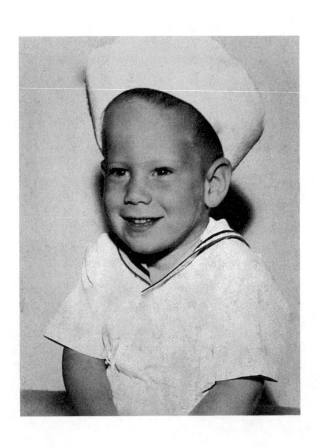

THREE

I have a job, a family, and several interesting hobbies. I read a lot, cook a fine jambalaya, and like to watch movies and TV. We entertain now and then, I've been known to clean the garage every few years, and sometimes we travel. In other words, like most people who traipse into the runners' realm, I knew that my first challenge would not be getting fit for running, but rather getting running to fit into my life. My career has always demanded long, strange hours incompatible with regularly scheduled exercise programs. So I crawled from bed bright and early the next morning, pulled on my running gear, and took Linda to breakfast.

"Shouldn't you be, you know, actually running," she asked as I leaned over my bacon, grits, and a steaming waffle at our favorite café.

"The schedule says I'm supposed to rest today."

"From what?"

"You want me to train properly, don't you?" I asked.

"Yes," she said slowly.

"Well, the schedule says I shouldn't start too fast."

"But you do have to start, don't you?"

"I started yesterday. Did you miss the part about resting?"

"Then why are you wearing running clothes?"

"Just getting used to the idea. You know what they say: 'Discretion is the better part of valor.'"

"What does that mean?"

"I don't know," I said. "I think it's a question."

"What's the question?"

"Are you going to eat that sausage?"

That's the problem with non-runners. They struggle to understand the finer points of the sport. Running is about more than just pounding the pavement. It involves sliding into the proper state of mind. Getting into the groove. You have to reach far down to find that delightful slice of Zen that comes only when you breathe deeply, your thighs burn, and your heart thunders. Sure, it sounds like sex, and that's no accident. In each case, you're having fun while getting sweaty. At least if you're doing it right.

The problem for most beginning runners is that the good times do not start until they are capable of running substantial distances. It is a paradox. Running nine miles is fun, and running three miles is work. Getting to the point where you can handle those longer runs takes weeks of drudgery, plodding through all sorts of weather, doing three-, four-, and five-mile loops.

The next morning I reluctantly took to the trail. The schedule called for four miles, and that seemed reasonable. It should have been, based on my past experience, but this plan included something that I had previously avoided like hunting trips with Dick Cheney.

"What's a TUT?" Linda asked as she attached my freshly printed schedule to the refrigerator with a magnet while I tightened my laces.

"Egyptian pharaoh. Is that exhibit touring again? You know, as dead guys go, he travels more than James Brown."

"No," she said. "It says, 'TUT, four minutes.' Right here."

Most married couples have one partner who glosses over the fine print and one who pays attention to details. I am the glosser, so I had ignored that notation. Now, however, being compelled to show how serious I was, I took a look. Sure enough, there it was: TUT.

"I have no idea. Maybe it means I should lie down on the side of the road like I'm dead."

"Here it is," she said. Dr. Fine Print struck. "It means 'total uphill time.' You're supposed to run uphill for at least four minutes during the four miles."

"Hmmm. All at once?"

"You can spread it out."

"Oh."

"But it should be done 'semi-vigorously.'"

It all sounded ominous, yet she followed me out the front door and gave me a cheery "Good luck!" as I headed to the street. "Remember, 'semi-vigorously'!"

TUTs aside, I was optimistic.

Some people come into this world with a gift for music. Some excel at mathematics. Some have a green thumb or can spot a bargain on eBay. I was born with a natural ability to run long distances faster than most people. Short races were anathema. In a race from one end of a football field to the other, I would end up in the middle of the pack, at best. But the longer the race, the more my position improved.

My mom and dad noticed this tendency in South Dakota, where I went to kindergarten. Racing tumbleweeds through the backyard or running across the playground, I opened up like a miniature pronghorn streaking over the Great Plains. That western antelope, by the way, is the second-fastest land mammal on the planet, ranking closely behind the cheetah; and since the pronghorn sustains its top speed for longer distances, some argue it is actually the faster critter. I didn't know all that at the time, but in retrospect I did have some things in common with that magnificent animal. Not only were we both fast, but also, just as pronghorns mark their territory with musk, sometimes I would sleepwalk through the house and pee in the linen closet.

We lived at Ellsworth Air Force Base, where my father served in the Strategic Air Command, ready to fill the sky with B-52s packed with nuclear bombs should the cold war suddenly get hot. And just as the vast, open landscape of the West seemed tailor-made for long runways and missile silos, it was also a perfect place for running. In every direction, the dusty earth extended unbroken to the horizon, fairly begging one to slip into a loping gallop.

Recesses and lunch periods at Badger Clark Elementary were spent racing up and down the playground. At home, my friends and I dashed back and forth to a large grassy field on the edge of the military base, flinging ourselves tirelessly across the turf. With an older sister, Chris, and older brother, Robert, I was always being urged to "keep up!" And in large part I did. Camping in the Black Hills a few miles behind

Mount Rushmore, I hardened my legs by chipmunking up and down mountains and by hiking with my family.

By the time I was in the third grade, my father had retired from the military, and we'd moved to Champaign, Illinois, where I was winning the school's annual Field Day race. It was a 300-yard rip around an empty lot in our working-class neighborhood, which was ironically named Holiday Park. I'd line up beside all the other kids, flexing my feet inside my black Keds, and then at the whistle I'd cut loose. My friend Patrick, whom I suspect had wagered a comic book on my winning, told me that I should sprint at the end. I didn't know what that meant, but "sprint" sounded like "limp," so as I turned into the home stretch, I shifted into a lunging, lopsided stride, one leg shooting ahead as I dragged the other. My teachers must have thought I was having a juvenile stroke, but I surged to victory anyway.

When I was in fifth grade, we moved again to another, much smaller town in Illinois. In Sullivan, I was no longer lurching like Igor. Indeed, my running in gym class soon had the school's track coach, John Ruskin, inviting me to be a distance runner with the eighth-grade team. I was nervous about being among the older kids, but from the first practice, my fears were allayed. I blasted off from the pack like my hair was on fire and never looked back. Within a few days they had all accepted me as a worthy contender. After a few meets it was taken for granted that I would beat all comers if the course was long enough.

It never occurred to me that rules might get in the way— specifically, a statewide rule forbidding anyone as young as I was to compete in any race longer than a mile. The rule actually made sense. Younger kids' bones and joints are still forming, and the repeated pounding of long-distance running can pose problems for some, producing nagging injuries that might hang around for years or for life. I suspect Coach Ruskin did not know much about the science of skeletal maturation in preteens, but like every phys ed teacher, he did know about rules. He was straight out of Central Casting: gray-haired, square-jawed, and sturdy. He called the shots and seemed thrilled that I was helping the team rack up wins, until we made it up into the higher competition of a regional meet. On the way to that contest, he summoned me to the front of the bus.

"I have you in the hundred today," he growled.

"The hundred? The hundred-yard dash? You're wrong, Coach. I'm in the two-miler."

"Nope, you're in the hundred."

"I can't run the hundred. I'm not a sprinter."

"Here's the deal," he said. "According to the rules, you're too young to be on the team. If you run the two-miler and win, the other coaches could start poking around, and if they find out you're running illegally, we'll have to forfeit every meet we won this year. I don't feel like cleaning out the trophy case. So you're running the hundred."

As much as I disliked it, in retrospect it was a great plan. Thrust into the foreign land of sprinters, I was hopeless. I rattled to the line with my adjustable metal starting blocks, fumbled with them for a few minutes, then tossed them aside. Everyone else had on track spikes. I was in slick-bottomed sneakers. The other runners were testing their starting strides by exploding forward a dozen yards to warm up their muscles and to establish a rhythm. I tried to do the same, slipped on the cinder track, and came down hard. My own teammate, a guy named Mitch who actually could sprint, stayed in his lane and pretended he didn't know me. The other runners looked on, trying to figure out if I was a ringer who would rocket out of a standing start to leave them in the dust or a hapless loser in the wrong place at the wrong time.

The mystery was blown away by the starter's gun. The others were gone before I made it out of my awkward crouch, spraying cinders and fighting for traction. By the time I hit the finish line, they were in the showers. My teammates, who were used to me destroying all challengers at greater distances, howled at my inability to make even a respectable showing. As far as Coach Ruskin was concerned it was mission accomplished. None of the other teams' coaches even raised an eyebrow.

I had to wait until high school, when the longest sanctioned races grew beyond two miles, to start doing what I did best on a routine basis. On my first training run with the small cross-country team, Coach Doug Dunagan, a long-haired Bill Bixby look-alike, pointed us down a country road through the soybeans and said he'd meet us in a while. By the time he caught up to us in his silver Camaro, we were miles outside town and I was far ahead of the others.

"Outstanding!" Coach Dunagan kept saying as we rode back, jammed into his car like a half-dozen sardines. He was excited not merely to have a fast long-distance man but also for that guy to be a freshman. It portended years of potential championships, and he was delighted.

At first, winning was easy. I would leap out in front in any meet and seize an insurmountable lead. Behind me, other contenders would try to hold on but invariably fall by the wayside as I set down a blistering pace. If someone tried to pull the same trick on me by dashing away from the start, I'd get on his heels and mercilessly hound him. Then, in the final half mile, when he would be overcome by fatigue, I'd blast by as if the race were just beginning.

This is a more impressive feat if you consider my training regimen. When classes let out each day and the team assembled on the football field, the sprinters and hurdlers would rip up and down one side of the track, refining their rhythm and explosive power. The high jumpers and pole-vaulters would saunter to the big mat in the end zone; the former flopping like salmon going upstream as they tried to clear the rising metal bar, and the latter charging like modern-day Don Quixotes with aluminum lances and launching themselves at the sky. The shot put and discus guys would lumber off to a concrete circle, to strain, and spin, and grunt as they forced chunks of metal to defy gravity. The other distance runners and I would disappear. The coach thought we were taking off into the Illinois countryside, building up our endurance by heading through the cornfields, past Angus cows, across creeks, and around tidy red barns. He assumed this because we would tell him so.

"How far did you go today, boys?"

"At least four miles. Maybe six."

"That's wonderful." And he'd write it down in his training book as if the news were given to him by the god Mercury in his winged shoes.

The truth was less inspiring, but more in keeping with teenage males. Sometimes we would run for extended periods (for example, there was that time we threw a rock and broke a window in the Boy Scouts meeting cabin), but more often we would just run until we were out of sight. Then we would walk around town, talk about girls, sit in the grass, and kill time until we figured we'd been gone long enough. Usually we'd sprint a few hundred yards just before the end to work up a sweat, and then we'd trot back and report on our session. Other times we didn't even do that much. We'd slip off to the old, discarded high-jump mats near the gym and flop down, disappearing into their soft foam. We'd pass the time chatting with cheerleaders and pom-pom girls until the whole team had hit the showers, leaving the coach to wonder whether we were still out there on the roads stacking up training miles. He must have admired our dedication.

And despite this dilettantish approach, I kept winning.

Before one meet, some opposing runners were confused about how the course wound through a maze of roads in the town park. Time and again my teammate and good friend Kendall Demaree tried to explain the route. Finally, he pointed at me and said, "Just follow him. He'll be in front anyway."

All wins. No work. There was nothing not to like in my plan.

That is, until I progressed into bigger meets where I met runners who were just as talented and who had trained. For the first time ever, I found myself seriously tested and my tricks were turned against me. If I went out front, my opponents dogged my heels. If I tried to draft off of them, they would drag me to the point of exhaustion and then pull away. I remember a race in which the entire field of opposing runners stretched out such a massive lead that I may as well have been running the next day.

I had a reprieve in my junior year of high school, when my family moved to Alabama. Bear Bryant's Crimson Tide was romping, and football was the undisputed king of sports, so in most places, high school track wasn't taken seriously. Once again, I treated my training with only a passing interest. During gym class at Opp High School, I would decide whether I liked the day's planned activity, and if the answer was no, I would tell the coach that I needed more time to run and would gently jog a loop of red dirt road behind the school. And when the races came around, I again captured victory after victory. I was undefeated in the handful of Alabama high school meets in which I participated. It was fun, easy, and boring.

The closest I came to losing was on a cross-country route that went from the track, across a parking lot, through the woods, and down a maze of paths and roads. I was far out front, but as we curved around to head back to the finish, I strayed off the poorly marked course. I was so far gone in the wrong direction that I could barely hear my teammates frantically calling me back. When I spied the new leader of the race, he was a quarter mile from the finish. I doubled back on my errant path, turned loose with everything I had, and caught him anyway, breaking the tape to cheers.

But by the time I went off to Troy State University, running was an occasional pastime. My roommate, Scott Strider, was an excellent cross-country athlete for the university, and occasionally I would join him for five or six miles, but that was it. While he arose before dawn to run, I slept. While he pounded through his evening training, I was acting in plays, or working at the town's radio station, or fiddling around in the campus TV studio. While he went off to compete against the best runners in the country, I hung out.

Still, shortly after my graduation, when I'd landed my first television reporting job at WSFA in Montgomery, my big brother called, and he had an unusual idea.

"Let's do the Vulcan Marathon."

Robert said this as if he were proposing a trip to Dairy Queen. He'd always been the superior athlete in our family. Ridiculously strong and as stubborn as a donkey, he excelled at every sport. In football, he was a one-man demolition squad. In basketball, he crashed the boards like a superhero. And in baseball, what he lacked in finesse he made up for in such great ferocity at the plate that I sometimes thought he scared the ball over the fence.

I could best him only in running, and then only if the distance was long enough. So, as the oft-victimized younger brother, I instantly suspected a trick in this invitation.

"What's the catch?" I asked.

"No catch. Let's just go run the race."

Marathons had become more popular in the running craze of the 1970s championed by Olympians Frank Shorter and Bill Rogers, author Jim Fixx, and others, but to me, the races were fearsome. The New York City Marathon was then a decade old, and in its inaugural had boasted 127 runners, less than half of whom finished. Even world-class marathoners talked of the pain, the exhaustion, and "hitting the wall." The Vulcan run was a monster. Starting atop Iron Mountain in the shadow of Birmingham's famous statue to the god of the forge (think the Statue of Liberty, only smaller, male, and more industrial), the marathon wound down into the suburbs, twisted around, and climbed from mile 12 to mile 20. The pitch to the summit was a brutal stretch of asphalt that came just as energy and will were evaporating. If you could clear the top, you faced a steep drop to the flats and an agonizing five miles to the finish.

But I did not think of that. I quickly calculated that it was Robert who had stumbled into the trap. Trying to show his athletic courage, he had proposed, I was certain, a test that he thought I would avoid. Then he could tease me endlessly about my cowardice without ever having to run the race himself. So I struck. "Sounds good to me!"

"Great," he said. "When you get time, swing by and I'll give you an entry form."

My bluff came crashing down around me. He was not kidding. His offer was for real, and I'd just agreed to it.

I knew it was a potentially dreadful mistake, and that was confirmed the next day when I dropped by to pick up the paperwork. Rather than prodding, teasing, or suggesting I wasn't up to the task, he offered a rarity among competitive brothers: genuine encouragement.

"This is going to be a lot of work," he said. "We need to be running every day, and long distances on weekends. Maybe we should try to get some hills in, or maybe some speed work. Make sure you write everything down in your runner's log so you can keep track of your progress. And you'd better not mess around about your training."

"What makes you think I would?" I asked.

"I saw you hiding in the high jump mats during track practice in high school."

"Oh."

"You need to come up with a plan and stick with it, because I don't really know much about these races, but I know they'll kick your butt if you don't watch it. And I don't want to be dragging you to the finish line."

"You'd do that for me?"

"No. So get busy."

With those words for inspiration, I began preparing more than I ever had before, which is to say that I started training for the first time in my life. I ran each evening. I ran on the weekends. I ran through neighborhoods, down country roads, in sun and rain, day and night. I ran every day for more minutes and more miles than I thought possible. At the time, some runners considered resistance training helpful, so I strapped weights onto my ankles. Encased in soft leather, each was filled with two pounds of small metal shot, and they made every step sound like I was smuggling a box of Tic Tacs in my socks. I felt as if I were running on a strange planet with increased gravity. Whether the weights made me stronger was debatable, although each time I took them off, I had that floating feeling you get after removing roller skates.

Our packets arrived in the mail some weeks later, with our race number, a T-shirt, and a big, colorful booklet filled with inspiring pictures of the Vulcan raising a piece of iron to the sky. There were glossy images of a crowded starting line, glowing volunteers, and happy runners chugging through the beautiful streets of Birmingham.

"This is inspiring," I told Robert, flipping through the pictures.

"Sure it is," he said. "They kept the autumn leaves in but left the puke shots out."

I'd been feeling pretty good about my longer runs, so I said, "I'm sure it won't be that bad."

"Don't kid yourself," he said. "Those last six miles are going to be tough."

"And the two-tenths!" I said, laughing.

"Yuck it up, funny boy."

We had mostly trained apart, but one week before the Vulcan, I joined him for our longest pre-race run. Frankly, it was our longest run ever: eighteen miles, most of it on a dusty logging road through pine forests. It went well. The distance flew by. Robert and I gushed about the race ahead, and as the sun set, our parents drove behind us in my dad's pickup to illuminate the road with the headlights. The benefits of training were wildly apparent, although I was unaware of the hidden danger in stepping up my mileage so quickly. Then, at mile 15, I got my first hint. We were bounding down an incline when my left knee crunched loudly enough for both of us to hear.

"That hurt," I said with a jittery laugh.

"Didn't sound good," Robert responded.

I wiggled my leg, testing the knee side to side as I kept moving. Other than some tenderness under the kneecap, it didn't seem like a serious matter. We finished the last few miles laughing and talking as if nothing had happened.

The next day, I knew something had. It was not a stabbing pain, but it was more than a tweak. It felt as if broken twigs were buried inside the joint. In the spirit of denial, I said nothing to anyone, piled on the ice, and stayed off my feet. I made no attempt at running.

We drove to Birmingham the evening before the race and

slept a fitful night in a cheap motel, before joining a few hundred other bleary-eyed runners on the mountain with the Vulcan lurking above. The morning dawned cool and clear, and the start was fine. The early miles were too. But by mile 10 my knee was bad. By 15 it was worse. By 21, after I'd crested the big hill, it throbbed like a toothache. I was barely moving. Then I wasn't. Then I quit.

The next year we went back. Once again, I was inadequately trained, but I avoided injury and hobbled across the finish line in a drenching rain. I limped around the TV station for the next three days, to the amusement of my news director, who had always assumed that I was a little off and now felt his suspicions were confirmed.

The next two years, Robert and I ran the Rocket City Marathon in Huntsville, and the pattern continued. I trained too little and deluded myself that it was too much. My personal best was around 3:44, gutted out on youth and will. Each race had been an ordeal. After that I hung up my marathoning shoes.

It was just as well. I met Linda, and after a couple of years of dating we began plotting marriage. She was a pharmacist by training, held an executive position with the Alabama Pharmacy Association, and was a rising national star in her field. My growing career was also demanding. There was no such thing as being off duty. Phone calls at all hours sent me to house fires, floods, airplane crashes, and murder scenes. I spent my days among protesters, prisoners, politicians, and some people who made it into all three categories, plus a seemingly infinite variety of other newsworthy souls. I moved to

WWL-TV in New Orleans, where eating softshell crabs, craw-fish étouffée, and oyster po'boys proved more interesting than chasing the streetcar down St. Charles Avenue.

I ran short races now and then, but in my decaying state of athleticism, they were no longer larks. One year, as I lumbered toward the finish line of the Crescent City Classic 10K, a woman I worked with named Janet spotted me boiling sweat and gaping like a catfish. "Oh my God," she yelled, making every head turn, "you are so pink!"

My days of running free, leaping onto the track without a care, and erasing miles with the stride of an antelope were over.

All of that, my entire running history, had drifted through my mind as I finished this first solo run of the new schedule I shared with Ronnie, trotting up to the front of our house some forty "semi-vigorous" minutes after I'd departed. I sat on the steps and breathed heavily, wondering whether she was having a better or worse experience in Atlanta.

"How was it?" Linda said as she came out to join me.

"Four miles down," I said. "Four hundred to go."

FOUR

To my relief, a few weeks later I was no longer enduring my runs but enjoying them. I ran before work in the crisp morning air. Late-autumn leaves swirled, Christmas tree lots popped up, and my time on the road took me away from worries about my job, shopping, and holiday preparations. It was still laborious, sometimes comically so, but even on days when the schedule called for rest, I found myself longing to run.

Ronnie came home for her winter break.

"You're running very well," I told her. We'd been talking on the phone every day, but this was the first time we'd run together since beginning our quest. As snowflakes pattered down around us, her stride was steady, her attitude positive.

"Thanks. You too. I've been honest about it."

"What do you mean?"

"I figure if running is a sport, it probably ought to have a few rules, and I've come up with some. Want to hear?"

"Okay. Shoot."

"First, we have to be honest," she said. "Just like you've always told me, 'Nothing good comes from self-deception.'" I didn't remember ever saying that, but since we were struggling up a hill and I could barely breathe, I let it pass. "Whatever the schedule calls for, that's what we have to do. If it says five miles, we have to run five miles, not a step less. If it says do short sprints, we do short sprints. And if it says run hills—"

"We run hills, I get it. Have you noticed that it always says 'run hills'?"

"Yeah. But I don't mind."

There was nothing to be said to that, of course. As a parent, I had learned that whenever a teenager voluntarily takes on a difficult task, it's a bad move to interfere. Teaching a child self-discipline is a serious undertaking. Seeing one rise to the challenge of her own volition was borderline amazing. "What other rules do you have in mind?"

"No whining."

"That's a gimme. Any more?"

"Even though it's just the two of us, we're a team," she said. "No one gets left behind."

"You mean like Lilo and Stitch?"

"Kind of. I think we'll run better if we run for each other instead of just for ourselves."

This was an interesting point, in part because I did not yet fully understand what she expected to gain from this experience. She was a hugely successful student. She was in the Maryland All-State Chorus. She taught tourists about the principles of flight at the Smithsonian National Air and Space Museum. Her model rocket team showed up for the national finals after their entry had been lost in the woods, and they constructed a new rocket on the spot from spare parts and equations scribbled on Ronnie's arm. They launched it seconds before disqualification and finished in the top ten.

That said, she'd struggled with all the typical issues of growing up: girlfriends who were unkind, boyfriends who were untrue, adults who were unfair, and adolescent days filled with uncertainty about her place in the world, her future, herself. Her maturity in handling these matters sometimes lulled Linda and me into thinking she was not bothered. Once, when she was in junior high, she came to talk to me about some social kerfuffle that had left her feelings bruised. I was distracted by work and snapped. "Listen, you've been through this before," I told her. "Get tougher, stand up for yourself, and quit complaining. I don't understand how you let this become a problem." She quietly nodded. Then, as she left the room, she turned from the doorway and said, "You know, I'm still a little girl."

But all those moments, even the hard ones, seemed to fit neatly into the person she was becoming. And the marathon did not. It was an outlier. Sports had never really been her thing.

Ever since her birth, I had been the dominant figure helping her develop her talents for running, jumping, wrestling, swimming, and skiing. Maybe I should have questioned her level of interest after she was thrown out of kiddie ski school for refusing to take a nap. But like any good-hearted father, I pressed on. I goaded her into many footraces, urging her to compete as hard as she could as I ran alongside, before lunging ahead to beat her at the wire. I remember Linda's reaction as I gloated. "What is the matter with you? Why didn't you let her win? She's seven years old."

"It's never too early to learn how to accept defeat," I'd say.

Now Ronnie was older and faster, and she seemed more dedicated to this task than she'd ever been to any other sport. As I considered her "no one gets left behind" rule, I decided it might play in my favor as the training went along.

"Deal," I said. "What else?"

"Oh God," she said.

"Praying? I can see that."

"No. Look." She pointed ahead. We had wound down to a dirt road alongside an old canal, with trees hanging over the water and big gray rocks jutting from the banks. The towpath is where mules walked as they pulled barges of coal to the nation's capital more than a century ago. The path is smooth, flat, and scenic. The woods teem with raccoons, foxes, herons, kingfishers, ducks, hawks, owls, the occasional bald eagle, and, at the moment, an unfortunate deer.

Or rather, an ex-deer. Its lifeless body was frozen in the canal, the neck twisting into the air where buzzards and crows had pecked at the head. A crimson stain had spread across the blue-white ice, and the snow was shrouding it in gauzy horror.

We stopped in respectful silence. Ronnie said, "How do you suppose that happened?"

"Probably tried to run across the road up there," I said, "got hit by a car, and limped down here."

"So, you think she broke through the ice and got stuck?"

"Looks like it."

"Poor thing. What a bad way to go," Ronnie said, turning to jog away as I fell into her wake. "Anyway, it's probably worth remembering."

"Why's that?"

"She was running."

Gruesome moments aside, I had my own hopes for this shared experience. Just as Ronnie was charting her course into the adult world and wondering where it would lead, I was feeling the anxiety of watching her go. The relationship we'd had all these years—daddy and daughter playing, talking, reading, singing, and cuddling together—was fading by the day. And I did not know what was arising in its place. It had occurred to me that running might hold an answer. If we jointly conquered this challenge, perhaps it would help define our new, more adult connection, drawing us closer in a different way. But I knew all too well that such grand plans can also end in failure. And what then? This experience could push us painfully, awfully, permanently farther apart. I considered this against the backdrop of one glaring realization that comes to any man with a house full of daughters: Men and women largely approach sports differently.

Until our daughters came along, I had been comfortably blind to the notion. I knew that I liked watching football and hockey more than Linda did. I also knew that she was not always as enthusiastic as I was about playing competitive sports. True, she was an assassin at backgammon, and she had run me ragged during one notable skiing season, but by and large she displayed limited interest in the "take no prisoners" games of boys.

When Ronnie was in grade school, I coached her soccer team. Having never played the game, I was a poor choice, and I spent the first practices figuring out the rules. I would have been better off figuring out the girls.

Ronnie was easy. She was tough and engaged, and she threw

herself headlong into every assignment. Put her in goal, and she would stare down attackers, even though she once took a ball in the face so hard that her nose spouted blood like a geyser. Put her on defense, and she would badger opposing strikers. Put her on offense, and she would drive to the net with a single-mindedness bordering on OCD. No matter what assignment I pushed her way, she tackled it with commitment and ferocity.

Some of the other girls also had talent and could maneuver around the field relatively well. I had no doubt that they could, on the right day, coalesce into a force to be reckoned with. Still, while my players were delightful, they were also puzzling. At the risk of sounding misogynistic, I can only say they were like girls.

In the small towns I'd known as a child, where the new attitudes of the raging 1960s washed in reluctantly from the cities, male culture held on to sports with a 1950s tenacity. Injuries were nothing. Winning was everything. There were no trophies for trying, at least not after peewee football. And a coach who bellowed at his team to run in the summer sun until they were delirious was at worst "tough" and at best "gruff but lovable." Girls' sports, when they existed at all, were seen as pale shadows of the male battlefields of football, basketball, baseball, and track.

Things had changed since then. I inherited my coach's position from the previous father who'd been drafted into it. I should have known something was up by the way he threw the box of orange field cones, practice jerseys, and clipboards at my feet and said, "Good luck!" His tone implied either "You're going to need it" or "I'd rather be beaten with a radiator hose than keep this job." I would have asked him for advice, but even if I'd yelled, he wouldn't have heard me over his squealing tires as he raced away.

The essential challenge was that coaching, at least for this team, was a lot like counseling. The girls had complicated relationships and a much more nuanced involvement with the game than I had anticipated. They could storm the field with unfettered enthusiasm one period and then mysteriously change gears the next, strolling around and chatting. Sometimes, when I urged them on with a Drew Brees–style speech, they would rise like warriors. Other times, they would shrug. Yelling at them to "Run!" when they didn't want to was like telling a fish to read poetry.

Best friends would inexplicably separate on the sidelines over some perceived slight, and a chill would descend on the whole team. New alliances would erupt over Friday-night pizza and cool into passive-aggressive islands of discontent by the starting whistle on Saturday. The game often seemed more like a by-product of their interactions rather than the main purpose. Once, a dog ran across the field mid-play at one of Ronnie's games, and all members of both teams left their positions to join in a joyful chase. Another time, a sideline discussion took on such intrigue that I could hardly persuade enough girls to take to the field to avoid a forfeit.

I don't say any of this in disrespect to them or their complicated approach to the sport. They could transform, without a hint of warning, into a soccer-playing juggernaut as fearsome as any ever conceived by boys, tearing through the other teams like paper. But while I knew how to inspire such moments in males, I never fully grasped what had spurred the girls' enthusiasm. I was a stranger in a strange land, and their relationship to me was a riddle. They were respectful and easy to get along with, and they seemed to genuinely like me.

"But every time I tell them to do something, they look at me like a bunch of cats," I said to Linda as we collected gear after a frustrating game in which the whole team acted disinterested to the point of narcolepsy.

"They're girls," Linda said. "They see things differently. If you can understand how they think, they will move mountains for you. But first, you're going to have to figure out which mountains motivate them."

"Yeah? I don't have that problem with Ronnie. She knows what I'm after, and she delivers every time."

Linda came over to put a hand on my shoulder. "Ronnie is your daughter. She is not playing this game because she loves sports. She's doing it because she loves you. You're her mountain."

Ronnie was perhaps the most tireless runner on her soccer team, but when she joined the high school cross-country team for one season, she struggled. Admittedly, it was a talented group with several girls who regularly threatened the runners in the state record books, but Ronnie wasn't used to being at the bottom of the pack in anything. Team practice found her trailing well behind the bulk of the varsity squad and ready to collapse by the time the team was dismissed for the day. Her races were physically and emotionally draining. Often, on the way to meets, I had to deliver pep talks while she clutched her stomach and hinted that she might get sick. More than once I had watched her pass by as I cheered her efforts at the back of the pack, and she had tears of disappointment welling in her eyes. By the time the season ended, I figured she'd been soured on running forever.

I told her, "It's no big deal. You stuck with the team from the beginning to the end. You should be proud of that."

She did not buy it. "I let you down."

"That's silly. No one says you have to be a good runner."

"You were a great runner."

"Were. Was. That was then and that was me. This is now and this is you. Don't worry about it."

Maybe she'd targeted the marathon for redemption, to prove to her coach, her teammates, and me that she could cut it. Not a bad thing, but I could only hope it would sustain her through the miles that loomed ahead. No matter how much you may want to run a marathon for someone else, part of it— maybe the biggest part—has to be for you.

In any case, we seldom talked of her cross-country experience now, and as the days of the year wound down, she appeared immersed in the joy of us running together. The whole family seemed to feel the excitement.

On Christmas morning, as we gathered around the tree, Linda, Ali, and Ronnie kept eyeing me as the gifts were opened and the pile was whittled down. They were blatantly steering me away from one bright package tucked under the branches in the back. Finally, Ronnie fished it out, beaming. It was from her, but the other two were in on the surprise. I looked at their expectant faces, untied the ribbon, tore through the paper, and opened the box. Nestled in sheets of red and green tissue was a new pair of shiny running shoes, the first I'd had in many years.

"I thought you could use them," Ronnie said.

"Try them on!" Ali chimed in.

"I got the size from the pair you're using now, so they ought to fit," Linda added.

They did. Perfectly. The blue and white uppers wrapped lusciously around my feet. The smooth laces slipped into tidy, clean bows. When I stood, the soles spread my weight softly against the floor. I walked across the room and understood the degree to which my old shoes had collapsed.

"Thank you, Ronnie. Thank you, all," I said. And they knew it was for more than the shoes. I was thanking them for encouraging me to tackle this seemingly impossible task, for tolerating the time it took, and for welcoming this new phase in our family dynamic. Linda and I were uniting around the cause, the way we had over many things for our kids. Ali was finding ways to time-shift her homework so if she needed help I would not be off training at the crucial moment. And despite whatever doubts I'd had about Ronnie's motivation, she was running every step with me, even when she was far away, and she was growing up with each mile. Our chats while running more often veered into introspection about school, her plans, her ideas, and her dreams. I loved every moment and looked forward to our runs like never before.

Ronnie and I ran on Christmas afternoon and every day through New Year's, and we discussed everything. All the caution of her teen years was gone. We talked about love and loss, about success and failure, and about the difference between what you hope for when you are young and what you settle for when you are older.

"Why did you stop running for all those years?" she asked as we eased through our final miles one afternoon.

"I was busy being a dad."

"You could have run too."

"I did. A bit. But when people say you have to figure out your priorities, they're right. You can be good at a lot of things, but you can't always be good at a lot of things at the same time. Running could wait. You couldn't."

"But I see how much you like this."

"I do. But I like you, your sister, and your mother more."

We often sprinted the last block at the end of our runs and collapsed into stumbles and wheezes as we celebrated the completion of that day's effort. We had just done that, wrapping up our final run of the winter break, and we were walking to cool off, panting and sweating. She came alongside me, linked her arm through mine, and said, "You know, you really are my hero." It will remain one of my best moments ever, and it gave me hope that this could indeed become about much more than just covering miles.

FIVE

*H*ow exactly did the marathon come to be such a strange distance?"

Ronnie posed the question on the phone. She was back at Georgia Tech, and we were chatting one evening in early January, comparing our workouts from earlier that day. I knew that the history of the marathon was much storied, revered, and utterly misunderstood, somewhat akin to the Taft administration. Like a lot of things related to Greece, it is so deeply rooted in history that it makes the rest of our civilization look like we started on it last weekend.

I also knew the short version. "A long time back, some Greeks were in a fight with some foreign invaders," I told her. "Maybe Canadians, I'm not sure. Anyway, the Greeks won, and this guy ran twenty-six miles to Athens to tell the king about it. Then he fell over dead. The end."

The story is simple, inspiring, and, as I discovered when I went googling later that night, probably not true. Or at least it is fuzzy in the details. Problem one: The tale was derived over hundreds of years from a variety of sources, some of whom may have been prone to exaggeration and heavy drinking.

Historians agree that back around 500 B.C., the Greeks did get into a fight with some visitors from afar. The Persians, like so many people long ago, were intent on taking over the known world, which was then about the size of Indiana. To do this, they needed to crush the powerful Greeks. So the Persians sailed to the shore near the plains of Marathon to engage them.

"Holy cow, will you look at all those ships!" the Greek generals said as the armada heaved into view. I'm using dramatic license, since we don't have any record of what they actually said, but certainly it had to be something like that. So one general said to another, *"Scairdy Catinus, don't you think we ought to send our fastest runner for help?"*

"Good idea, Cowardius! Call Pheidippides."

Problem two: We don't know much about this guy. We're not even sure of his name. It was either Pheidippides or Phillippedes, or possibly Steve. For our purposes, we'll stick with Pheidippides. Legend holds that he was a herald, which was the closest thing they had to a professional runner. Heralds were what the ancient folks relied on when they needed to communicate quickly over a long distance. Today, we would call them cell phones.

"Ah, Pheidippides, so good of you to drop by," the top general said. *"You may have noticed a bunch of menacing Persians hanging out at the marina, and that's what we need to talk about. We're thinking we could use some help keeping them from burning our buildings, destroying our crops, enslaving our people, and wiping us off of the earth. And you know who we'd like on our side?"*

"The Spartans?" Pheidippides replied.

"Well done! Would you mind trotting over to Sparta and asking them to lend a hand?"

Pheidippides took off on a 140-mile jaunt to summon the champion steel-cage death-match all-pro fighters of the day. In Sparta, he found bad news.

"We're sorry you ran all this way," the Spartans told him, *"but we're kind of tied up right now. See, we're having a religious festival. We already have the decorations in place. We sold raffle tickets. We bought a ham. And all this potato salad will be wasted if we don't eat it now. Mayonnaise in this heat? You know what I'm saying."*

Pheidippides ran all the way back to the battlefront, delivered the bad news, and joined the fight. How he did this after covering close to 300 miles in two days is anyone's guess, but perhaps he and the rest of the Greeks had unknown strength, because, although greatly outnumbered, they kicked the hell out of the invaders.

"How about that? I never thought we'd win!" the top guy said. *"Let's call Pheidippides again and have him carry the news back to Athens."*

Problem three: We have reached the central part of the legend in which this great runner, bursting with joy over this fantastic news, runs himself to death to deliver it to Athens. It is not clear that this ever happened. Other versions say that the whole army marched to Athens. Still other versions suggest they all went bowling.

I have not even mentioned the minor distraction of Pheidippides' allegedly bumping into the god Pan during all this scurrying. Legend has it that Pheidippides pledged his allegiance to Pan, and the half-goat deity rewarded him by magically appearing on the battlefield, scaring the bejeebers out of the Persians and giving birth to the word *panic*.

Despite all these improbable tales and hallucinations, the legend of the sandal-clad hero had staying power. As the centuries passed, it became rooted in the global public consciousness, and when the modern Olympics came onto the stage in the late 1800s, who should leap from the dust of history but the intrepid Pheidippides. Olympic organizers needed a centerpiece for their games—an event that not merely evoked athletic prowess, courage, and endurance but also echoed ancient Greek heritage. The marathon was perfect.

Which is not to say that fledgling marathons were flawless.

In its earliest incarnations, the race was a grab bag of distances, expectations, and skill levels. In the first Olympic marathon, only a few dozen runners competed, a fair number did not finish, and even the winner stopped for a glass of wine along the way. Presumably he figured that Pheidippides, with his whole routine of collapsing and dying at the finish, was a shade overzealous. Today, we know better. Pheidippides was just undertrained.

The race was usually about 25 miles, in a tip o' the hat to the distance between Marathon and Athens (which is actually 27 miles—go figure), but sometimes it was longer, and sometimes shorter. There was no focus on world records or medal counts. Each race was between the competitors on hand and no one else, so what difference would it make if they ran an odd distance? Then in 1908 a single race in London changed the marathon forever.

Organizers of the Olympics there had agonized over the racecourse. They wanted the marathon to start in an auspicious spot, wind through town in an entertaining fashion, and end in the Olympic stadium 25 miles later. That's 25 miles, not 26.2. But as racecourse architects have discovered ever since, these things get tricky, what with all the road closings, spectators, and Port-o-Lets. In jolly old England, last-minute problems included complaints about cobblestone roads, reviewing platforms that blocked the course, and a most important request that the race end exactly in front of the British Royal box so that King Edward VII and the Buckingham Palace gang would get a good look at their native-born champions and all the sweating foreigners. The royal family was wrestling with rising issues of socialism, women's rights, and labor disputes, so it seemed a small favor to grant. Doing so, however, along with accommodating all those other impediments along the course, lengthened the tidy 25-mile race to 26.2 miles.

And into that logistical maelstrom stepped a tiny Italian named Dorando Pietri, who had hoped to be a hometown favorite. He would have been, had Mother Nature played along. The Olympics were scheduled to be in Italy that year, where maybe the mileage would have worked out to a less awkward distance, but an uncooperative volcano named Vesuvius had other ideas. Italy had to surrender the games, England scooped them up, and Pietri found himself on the visitors' team. In his younger days, Pietri had been a candy shop worker. Then he discovered that he had a talent for running great distances much faster than his fellow Italians. He started entering races and became a sensation. He built up his running résumé with win after win, and shortly after the turn of the century he was ready to take on the world's best runners on the banks of the Thames.

When the gun sounded for the mid-afternoon start, brave little Pietri took off with fifty-six others. It was crushingly hot, and he spent the first half of the race trotting in the back, biding his time. As the miles clicked by, the heat bit hard, and the others began to drop. Pietri surged forward. Soon he was in second, chewing at the heels of the leader from South Africa. Then even that man fell to Pietri's furious assault. The Italian's lead grew wider and wider. By the time he entered the stadium to the roar of seventy-five thousand fans, not one challenger was in sight. All Pietri had to do was cruise through a salutary lap and collect his medal. In those final steps, however, the heat came to roost on his head too. Pietri began staggering. He grew disoriented and headed the wrong way. He stumbled. He fell. Five times. Some fans rushed forward, helped him to his feet, and pushed him in the right direction. Pandemonium reigned as the crowd watched Pietri's agonizing struggle, fearful that at any moment another runner would burst into the stadium and steal the championship.

Finally, Pietri fell across the line in first place, with the American runner Johnny Hayes coming in second. The victory celebration was short. The games had already been marked by bitter quarrels over the rules and how the flags of various nations were displayed, so no one was surprised when the American team protested that Pietri had been unfairly assisted by those well-meaning folks at the end. He had not finished on his own, as required. The officials agreed. He was disqualified, and Hayes took the gold.

But the distance Pietri covered in his heroic effort was to be enshrined as that of the official marathon: 26.2 miles. It has remained that way ever since. For an average man, the race requires well over twenty-three thousand steps—enough to make the least of runners bow to its might, and to make even the best respect it. And for all our sports science, technology, training, and nutrition, the marathon remains a contest of supreme simplicity.

The distance, the history, and the strategies have changed. The formula for success never has: Step to the road, bend your knees, and run.

SIX

*R*unning has a way of humbling you. My best runs have almost always been followed by worse ones. Each pain-free gallop down the road with songbirds winging alongside has been matched by an agonizing grind in which every muscle and joint howls to the heavens.

"You must be blessed with great knees," friends at work said as I gradually let them in on my plans with Ronnie.

"You'd think so," I'd say, waiting until they turned their backs before limping to my office. Some days my knees hurt, and some days my hips. On bad mornings, my ankles throbbed above my shoes, and my toes cringed inside. On occasion, my arms ached, and my chest felt torn apart at the hinges. My leg muscles, even as they grew harder and bigger, burned with lactic acid around the clock. I would sit at my desk feeling vaguely feverish from constantly pushing my muscles to the tearing point, giving them a day's rest, then pounding them again. A quick call for me to get to the studio brought a teeth-clenching dash up two flights of stairs.

At first, I tried to keep Linda in the dark. I bought an analgesic sports cream, which I hid in a bathroom drawer. After workouts, I would shower and then, like a guy sneaking snorts of schnapps, slather it on. The relief was immediate and much appreciated, but it came with a side effect. The cream smelled like a dozen nurses washing their hands.

"Are you chewing gum?" Linda asked one day after walking in just as I stashed my supply.

"No. I never chew gum. Why?"

"Something stinks. Did you get new deodorant?"

"No. I mean yes. That must be it."

"Well, like I said, it stinks."

"Really? I think it smells nice. Refreshing and clean."

"I'm sure you do," she said. She turned to leave, and then, with the faintest pharmacist's smile, she added, "It probably makes your knees feel better too."

I don't know why I thought she might use my suffering as an excuse to make me ease up. She'd previously balked at only a few of my more extreme ideas. She'd argued against my taking up skydiving weeks after we'd moved from Denver to Washington, suggesting she'd suffered enough nerve-frazzling excitement without my augering toward the ground at 120 miles an hour. On an adventurous vacation, she'd convinced me that taking an airplane out of the Ecuadoran jungle to be back in our hotel by evening would beat boarding a bus full of locals and chickens for a perilous three-day trek on a dirt road over the Andes. That sort of thing.

But as a strong cyclist in her own right, she accepted the necessity of my physical struggles. Maybe she was seeing, just as I did, the positives amid the negatives. I was sleeping more soundly and hopping out of bed with more vigor. My eyes were brighter, and my face had a healthy flush. I was eating well, and yet my weight was dropping. Even as my joints crackled like a sugarcane bonfire, for most hours of most days I felt better than I had in years.

I was also relearning a lesson from my youth: Whether something is uncomfortable or unpleasant has no bearing on whether it should be done. The decision and commitment must be made, if not heedless of the pain, then at least with recognition that sometimes good things require bad days.

Of course, even that fortune-cookie approach was not enough to prepare me for what came next. A couple of weeks after Ronnie went back to classes, something terrible happened. Winter came. Not the "Frosty the Snowman" or "warm woolen mittens" winter we'd been experiencing for a few weeks already, but the eye-watering, throat-burning, nose-biting arrival of the kind of serious cold that drove the dinosaurs to extinction and made Neanderthal man learn to knit sweaters.

I knew the arrival of winter was real, because Mitt Romney told me so.

I was in New York as part of CNN's coverage of President Barack Obama's State of the Union address. The speech was that night, but my training schedule called for six miles that morning, and a storm system was cruising the Eastern Seaboard, leaving horrific snowdrifts, downed power lines, and arctic temperatures.

I woke in the Empire Hotel, a block off Central Park, and looked out the window at a postapocalyptic, iced-over Manhattan. Visions of the frozen deer from the canal congealed in my brain. Nonetheless, I pulled on my running gear, a layer of spandex winter wear, and then another layer. I jammed a stocking cap over my head and wrapped a scarf around my neck and face. I slid on my favorite running gloves, a six-dollar pair emblazoned with the emblem of my beloved New Orleans Saints. Then I pulled another pair of gloves over them. Down the hall, I punched the elevator button and stepped in to find that the only other passenger was the former governor of Massachusetts.

Romney looked me up and down, alighted on the thin slit through which my eyes were blinking, and smiled that weird political smile. He said, "You're not going to run in these conditions, are you?"

I answered, "I think I should ask you that question."

He chuckled in a way that said "*Okay, crazy,*" but when I hit the street, no one was laughing. The wind shrieked between the buildings. The drifts dragged at my feet. My eyelashes froze, and my exposed skin was scoured in a slipstream of horizontal ice crystals. My first breath crackled into my lungs. By the time I reached the far side of the park, my feet were frozen and my fingertips had no feeling. I saw a woman in a ponderous coat calling for her dog and watched it pop up from a drift like an icy jack-in-the-box.

Who the hell walks a dog in weather like this? I thought. The look she gave me betrayed her similar thought: Who the hell runs on a day like this? I slipped and slid my way through the empty zoo, past the boathouse, behind the Metropolitan Museum of Art, and around the reservoir. By the time I burst into the hotel lobby, dragging my own personal cold front and spraying snowflakes, all romantic illusions about my winter runs ahead were gone.

Back in my room, I sat on the bed and looked at my training schedule. Six-mile runs would soon turn into nine-milers, which would jump to twelve-, fourteen-, and sixteen-milers. My time outdoors would go straight up, while the temperature went straight down. I did my part covering the president's speech that night in an icy fog of fear. And the storm kept blowing.

"My God," Linda said when I was back in D.C. We had just awakened, and she was looking out our bedroom window at our frozen neighborhood. "I don't think you're going anywhere today."

"How bad is it?" I asked.

"You'll need a snowmobile."

I dragged myself out of the warm bed to join her. The world was whiter than a David Duke barbecue. Snow was still falling, and blowing into great, sweeping waves. The only thing more impressive was the arch in my wife's eyebrows when she saw me pulling on my running gear anyway.

"You can't be serious," she said. "How far do you think you'll make it?"

"The schedule calls for eight miles."

"That's not what I asked," she said.

"Yeah, but that's the answer."

"No way."

That sounded like a challenge, and I took it. Minutes later, I was wishing I hadn't. I had started with the idea that I would simply run as if there were no snow. I would follow one of my regular courses, lift my feet a little higher, and, Bob's your uncle, I'd be done in an hour. Instead, a quarter mile down a bike path, I was digging through snowbanks like an Iditarod dog and barely moving. I switched strategies, cutting toward a small national park near our home. At the entrance, a park ranger was running a snowblower in arctic wear suitable for Anchorage.

"Sorry, the park is closed," he said.

"Closed? But I need someplace to run."

"How about a treadmill?"

"Don't have one. I need eight miles."

"I need to win the lottery. I guess we're both screwed."

The drifts on the trail behind him looked too deep anyway. I turned around and pounded back toward the house. Sweat poured down my face, forming a frosty rime on my chin. I was blowing locomotive breaths and had covered less than a half mile. A snowplow rumbled past in a shower of white, and in a fit of inspiration I jumped into its wake. The plow led me to a neighborhood where other plows had been at work, wallowing out enough ruts to make the roads passable. Dodging occasional cars, slipping wildly, and gritting my teeth, I knocked the miles down. It took much longer than eight miles should, but when I returned home—my body crusted with ice and my feet encased in snowballs—my wife opened the door and slow-clapped my arrival.

"Very impressive," she said. "Now, don't drip on the floor."

I should have seen it coming, as Ali reminded me later that same day when I was pulling my running gear from the dryer. "Say, Dad, have you ever noticed what happens with the weather every year around this time?"

"It gets cold."

"Correct! And have you noticed what most people do when it gets cold?"

"They stay inside."

"Correct, again! So, when you agreed to run this marathon with Ronnie, did it not occur to you that this plan could put you into something of a tight spot, vis-à-vis doing what normal people do?"

"No, Ali, to be honest, it never did."

"I could tell you that my love will keep you warm," she smiled, "but I'm not sure that will do the job."

She was right, of course. I had overlooked a basic fact that even a novice runner should have caught: A spring marathon means winter training. For Ronnie in Atlanta, it was no big deal. Her days were chilly now and then. But I ran in stinging sleet and blistering blasts of snow, in the subzero light of morning and the bone-cracking black of night. I ran with tiptoeing steps over patches of braised frost, and with heavy strides smashing through stands of ice. I ran in weather that would have made Admiral Peary despair.

Every day Ronnie called to check on my progress.

"How's it going?" she'd say, sunshine seeping through the phone.

"All right. I ran into a group of Inuit yesterday. They were camping."

"Ha! Good one. But seriously, how is it?"

"Not bad. The caribou migration is slowing me down, but otherwise . . ."

"Another good one! Clearly winter is treating you well."

"It's okay. If I can only avoid the polar bears . . ."

She helped me lament the worst moments and pushed me

to enjoy the best. She told me about little things she'd seen on her runs and asked me about my own. I offered technical advice when it was needed; she gave encouragement when it was wanted. The sun remained nowhere to be seen. And day by day, the training schedule's little squares were filled in with yellow highlighter.

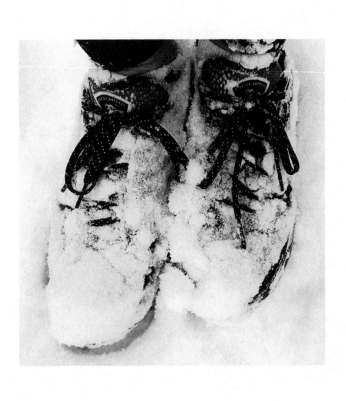

SEVEN

As winter dragged, my mileage soared.

"Seems to me that you are out there much more time than you were a few weeks ago," Ali said as I drove her to school.

"I am."

"I mean, a couple of months ago you were just gone for thirty minutes or so when you went running, and now it's like you're gone for hours."

"Like I said, I am."

"You're not sneaking away to cheat on Mom, are you?"

"I could find easier ways."

"I'll take your word on that. You look like an Otter Pop when you come back inside."

"As always, thanks for your support."

"The red ones."

She gave me a quick hug and hopped out. I watched her disappear into the building, surrounded by classmates, and I was grateful for her cheerful, chiding encouragement. Like Ali, I had been the youngest child in my family. And I knew that out of all the people in the house, she was getting shortchanged the most by my training. She was easygoing, quick with a joke, and always ready to take care of herself when her older sister, the house, the cars, or the dog demanded her parents' immediate attention. Sometimes Linda and I feared that she was independent to a fault. Too often we learned after the fact that she'd been bullied, or was struggling with a class, or simply felt lonely and we had missed the signs. Ali never complained. She forged ahead, finding solace in music, watching comedians on YouTube, and prodding us into occasional late-night runs to Krispy Kreme. The doughnuts didn't matter; she wanted the ride—the time in the car with just us, talking about movies, TV shows, and things she'd read.

As I wheeled away, I made a mental note to spend a little extra time with her.

It was a rest day. The warm car, the murmuring radio, and the slow start were seductive reminders of how easy my life was before taking up Ronnie's offer to run. That past weekend, I had once again nearly seen the whole manic scheme come off the rails when I found myself unexpectedly in the South Pacific. Or, I should say, at *South Pacific*. The classic Broadway musical was touring, and Linda had given her brother and his wife tickets to the matinee at the Kennedy Center. Ken and Eva drove down from Jersey, and we all loaded into our car. On the way to the show, I tried to keep up with the conversation about jobs, the kids, and our plans for later in the year, but my mind was on the trail.

The temperature had been below freezing for days, and the canal path was covered with snow and ice. In the daylight I could manage it well enough, but if I started after dark with the chill tightening my muscles and straining my endurance, it would be treacherous. I took one last look at the sun as we drove into the underground parking garage, and I hoped for a short show with no curtain calls.

We found ourselves in box seats a short distance from the then secretary of Homeland Security, Janet Napolitano. It was an interesting Washington moment. During an intermission, she and I exchanged pleasantries, the way journalists and public officials do, but my mind remained elsewhere when the program resumed. Onstage, people were prancing through enchanted evenings and singing about washing men out of their hair. I was squirming and imagining how precious minutes of comparative warmth and daylight were evaporating. By the time we made it through the ovations and were on our way home, the sky was streaked with hints of evening's purple. The mercury was falling fast.

Awaiting me were fourteen miles, and there was no way I could cover them. Dinner would take two hours. Good-byes and driving home another half hour. I would be launching into pitch-blackness and shattering cold. Despite not having missed a single mile since training began, I did not see how I could make it work. It was just that simple. My will was wilting, and I feared that if it collapsed this one time, I was done.

I don't much like the way people throw around superlatives these days. Seems like every character who rescues a cat, runs out of a burning building, or stands up for a cause after it's won somehow gets tagged as "extraordinary." But what my wife did at that moment made her exceptional to me. She'd been looking forward to the evening out with her brother and sister-in-law for months. She was having a great time and in no hurry for it to end. Yet she selflessly did something for which I will always be grateful.

She saw the agony on my face as we passed the Watergate building, with Georgetown rising bright and beautiful beside the river. Her hand slipped across the front seat and squeezed mine. "Hey, Ken and Eva, Tom has some important training that he ought to do this evening. It's a long run, and if he doesn't start now, he'll be out there past midnight. I will be worried sick. Do you mind if we let him go and we have dinner as a threesome?"

A quarter hour later, I had dashed inside, changed, and was back out the door, ripping down the asphalt in the twilight. Five miles after that, I cut off the road and onto the towpath. The sun was gone and darkness reigned. The thermometer was diving, but I didn't care. The miles literally slid beneath me as my shoes skidded across the ice. It should have terrified me. "If you fall out there and get hurt," Ronnie had told me a few weeks earlier, "no one is going to find you." She was right. After a certain hour in this cold, no one ventured down onto these trails, and if they did, they were not the kind of people you would want to encounter. It didn't matter. I slammed forward, pounding my feet down to secure my tracks.

With concentration and steady effort, I found that I could minimize the instability enough to make progress. Still, running blind was nerve-racking. Maybe it was the lateness of the day, fatigue from sitting in the theater, the temperature, or everything at once, but by the turnaround at mile 7, my enthusiasm was waning. I was exhausted.

I slowed to a stop at the end of a bridge sandwiched between a big stand of rocks and a wide spot in the canal. It was a lovely place on a summer afternoon, but in these circumstances it was bleak and spooky; I could have been the last person on earth. My legs were quivering. Sweat frosted my cheeks. I looked up into the infinity of space, and I felt the cold clawing deeper into my clothes and under my flesh. I needed to move again, but having stopped to consider the moment, the trip back through the blackness was even more intimidating.

A church bell pealed across the river in Virginia. Tree branches creaked, and even with no wind, twigs chattered against the bitterness. Far away, in some direction I could not fathom, a police siren rose once, twice, and faded. The hiss of distant traffic whispered.

I exhaled a rolling cloud of condensation and leaned back to watch it obscure the stars. Finally I beat my arms back and forth to generate some heat, took a few tentative steps, and began running again. The fatigue was multiplied by my apprehension, and I was dreading the next hour when I caught a break.

I hadn't previously noticed the full moon creeping over the horizon just behind the trees, and at that moment, it burst into sight, luscious and startling in its brightness. It illuminated the snow as if someone had turned a switch, spilling into the valleys formed by the trees, filling the woods with pale light. I couldn't see every detail, but I could see so much more than I was able to just minutes earlier. The canal was a shimmering sheet. The trail was a bright ribbon through the brush. I opened my stride, aiming for crusts of snow where the footing was surer. My pace remained cautious but was more confident.

A shadow shot from the woods, paused, and bolted into the brush. A fox on a late prowl. When I came closer to the river, I could hear it gurgling around frozen outcroppings.

My feet crunched on, each step quicker. Mile 9. Mile 12, 13. All the fear and isolation were vanishing, pushed aside by glorious, freewheeling exertion. I knew I could still fall, but somehow I also knew I would not. Not this night. Not on this trail. My strides came effortlessly, and my breathing was silky. An owl hooted. House lights appeared on the ridges as I closed in on home.

The bridge leading up to my neighborhood loomed unexpectedly in the moonlight. I crossed the canal, puffed up the hill, rounded the last corners, stumbled through the front door, and collapsed on the mat.

"Hey, the Otter Pop is back!" Ali called from the family room, where she was curled up on the sofa with homework. A rush of heat burned my face, and for a moment I wished I were back outside. I pulled my gloves and hat off with red, icy hands and sat there with steam rising from my hair, my glasses fogging over. I fell back on the floor, drawing deep breaths, succumbing to the shock of all that effort in all that cold. My head seemed to be ringing from the quick temperature change. Turned out it was the phone.

"Hi, Ronnie," I heard Linda say as she walked my way from the kitchen. "He just came in. Hey, Jack London, it's your daughter."

I fumbled the phone to my ear.

"Hi, sweetie. How is Atlanta?"

"A lot warmer than where you are."

"I guess. I'm pretty frozen."

"I have something that will help."

"What's that?"

"A wonderful idea."

EIGHT

Music thumped along the shores of the Mississippi River. Seventeen thousand runners rumbled and surged in the starting corrals, and the first wave exploded onto the course. The Rock 'n' Roll Mardi Gras Marathon and Half Marathon was under way, and Ronnie and I were in the middle, quick-stepping our way through the tight crowd, hopping over piles of clothing dropped at the last moment in the chilly dawn, and hollering out to famed Olympian Frank Shorter on the starter's stand, "Forgive us, Saint Frank, for we are runners!"

He laughed, and we sprinted away in our first official race since launching our plan. It was Ronnie's first half marathon ever.

"How are you feeling?" I asked a quarter mile in. The question was not as premature as it may have seemed.

"I'm good!" she said with a wide smile.

We'd started our race a half hour earlier. This was the core of Ronnie's great idea. Our training schedule called for sixteen miles on this Sunday. Her proposal on the phone that bitterly cold day weeks earlier was that our whole family fly to New Orleans. She and I would run three miles, reach the starting line in time for the gun, and take off for another 13.1 miles. So we had tumbled out of our downtown hotel ahead of dawn and set off in a brisk wind, cutting across Canal Street, down Royal, and through the heart of the French Quarter as bartenders hosed the sidewalks after one of the endless nights of revelry that define the city. Antiques and fine art glowed in some shop windows, while in others T-shirts festooned with fake boobs waited for tasteless tourists. We whipped by the Clover Grill, part of the passing scene in the 1966 film *This Property Is Condemned*. Boutique hotels beckoned with leaded-glass doors and gas lamps. Wrought-iron balconies hovered overhead. Turning at Esplanade Avenue, we headed down through the French Market, where the vendors were laying out bracelets, cookbooks, necklaces, and lacquered alligator heads. I've never needed urging to go watch the sunrise in the French Quarter, and this was a good reminder of why. An orange glow had spread over the Mississippi, boiling up a low fog on the surface of the water, and it promised to be a great racing morning: warm enough to run free and fast, but cool enough to not overheat.

Skipping past Jackson Square and a handful of early café au lait fans shaking powdered sugar from their beignets at Café Du Monde, we traced the riverfront. The steam-powered paddle wheeler *Natchez* rocked in its moorings, and the Aquarium of the Americas waited for opening hour. The great steel bridge to Algiers rose ahead, high above the muddy expanse of river. We had run past the Morial Convention Center, joined the other runners right on time, and the race was on.

I had been looking forward to it ever since Ronnie raised the idea, because I knew from my years living in the Crescent City that anything that is fun anywhere else is twice as fun here. The Rock 'n' Roll race series puts a premium on the overall experience of running by arranging for live bands, great aid stations, solid swag, and lots of cheering crowds in its tour stops throughout the United States and Europe. Here the organizers hardly had to bother. New Orleanians are drawn to parties like mosquitoes to hurricane lanterns. In addition to the official bands, clusters of musicians appeared on street corners, porches, and balconies just because they wanted to. In New Orleans even bad musicians are pretty good, so the tunes pouring into the morning light were inspired and inspiring: jazz, rock, blues, country, zydeco, and even a smattering of old Dixieland.

A higher-than-average percentage of runners were in costume, adding to the carefree atmosphere. Fairies, superheroes, clowns, and angels darted through the crowd as if Mardi Gras, still weeks away, were already in full swing. And of course there were the folks wearing shirts that promoted Bible verses, or charitable causes, or just their own past runs.

"What is the Mojave Death Race?" Ronnie asked as a guy trundled past at mile 3 wearing a frayed T-shirt sporting its logo.

"Must be in California," I said. "Sounds tough."

The shirt looked old, and the race intimidating. I'd been to the Mojave Desert, and it struck me that running in that natural furnace could go hand-in-glove with an early demise. I would learn later that the Death Race was a 250-mile bygone relay race that fed off an earlier running craze. Whether this guy had actually participated, I couldn't say. He looked the part of a "run bum," broken down in the knees, chuffing along with a bowlegged shuffle, his skin leathery from sun and wind, with a threadbare bandana around his head and tattered shoes on his feet.

"Give him some room," I advised Ronnie. I wasn't sure he was dangerous, but the evidence suggested that he was almost certainly crazy.

We slipped past him and found plenty more to attract our attention, including an outrageous moving buffet of snacks and beverages. This requires a little perspective to appreciate. In my marathons long ago, I had been lucky to encounter two or three aid stations in the entire 26.2 miles, and all they had was water. In a strange way, even that was frowned upon. Elite runners knew they had to drink to stay alive, but an awful lot of folks in my part of the pack back in the 1980s would blow past anyone who offered a paper cup with haughty looks that said, "*Oh sure, anyone can run a marathon if he has water. But I'll do it without so much as a sip! Now, step aside, weenies!*" They would finish without a drop of sweat left, their tongues as dry and thick as tennis balls, and bragging about how they were urinating blood. Still, the aid stations were so limited even those of us who took advantage of them weren't getting much more help.

Since then, the level of support in all races, especially long ones, has grown exponentially. Modern runners are offered water and sports drinks, sometimes two or more flavors, every few miles. High-energy gel packs are handed out along with orange slices and bananas. Medical stations with everything from Ace bandages to aspirin are seldom more than a few minutes away. In New Orleans, just as with the music, the local population raises the bar even higher in terms of in-race nutrition. Smiling folks stood by the course every few blocks offering the breakfast of champions.

"Hey, get some Popeyes fried chicken here!"

"Grab a doughnut!"

"Po'boys!"

"Have some king cake!"

We rounded a corner at mile 5, and there was a guy in a tuxedo holding a tray of brightly colored drinks. "Martinis! Shaken, not stirred!"

"Should I grab one?" Ronnie asked. "I'm pretty thirsty."

"No."

"Why? Because it'll slow me down to be drunk?"

"Because you're eighteen."

"This town is a riot," Ronnie said.

Her humor was a good sign. The half marathon is a potentially deceptive and damaging race. For people who run marathons regularly, it is something of a lark. They knock out 13.1 miles like Beyoncé churns out hits. If they are pushing for a PR, a half marathon may tax them, but there is no doubt about finishing. This is one reason public interest in half marathons has exploded. These races allow aging runners to feel as if they are still in the game with minimal risk of humiliation. If you have a bad time, you can shrug it off: "I was just running for fun." If you finish well, you can brag about it, and because the word *marathon* is in the race title, non-runners will take notice. But for new runners who see the half as a stepping-stone to the full marathon, it can be a monkey trap: something they can grab hold of only to find it is their undoing.

In any big race, it's easy to get caught up in the excitement of the early miles, and half marathons are brilliantly constructed for this mistake. They start in the early morning. Everyone is pumped. Many in the crowd are running the longest race of their lives with dreams of tackling an even longer one in the near future. The applause and music urge everyone on. A few runners get overeager and blast away as if they've knocked off a liquor store. More follow, and pretty soon running mass hysteria or "rip-nosis" takes over. Thousands of people who have never managed fewer than ten minutes per mile in training find themselves tearing along under a nine-minute pace. They forget about splits, pacing, and conserving energy. All they think is, "I must go faster to keep up with everyone else! *Aghh!* That guy is passing me!"

In their mania, many think they look like serious racers, but they more closely resemble extras in a *Godzilla* movie, and almost nothing can bring them to their senses. By mid-race, they are light-headed and sucking air. By ten miles, they are staggering and losing time fast. By the finish line, they may well be heaving up power bars and Gatorade, clutching their sides, and reconsidering the whole notion of a full marathon. In the worst cases, it can be an ugly end to months of training.

The flip side is less common, but also a race ruiner. Some beginners are so cautious that they run too slowly. They putter along, terrified of not finishing, and end up hardly moving. They fall so far back that they are miserably disappointed with their finish time, and just like their too-fast brethren, they also wonder whether attempting a full marathon would now be a big mistake. It's a shame. It's also one of the best reasons for novice runners to pair up with someone more experienced, who can talk them down from the "too fast" ledge or up from the "too slow" pit.

And it occurred to me around mile 9 that this was the job I needed to fill for my daughter. Although my own performance was hardly guaranteed, I had at least been in this territory before. I knew how the final section would feel. Never mind that only a mile back I'd dashed to a medical tent seeking Band-Aids for my nipples, which were chafing against my shirt so much they were bleeding. I had to be the guy in charge.

Thankfully, it did not seem difficult. As we passed under a giant, inflated Rock 'n' Roll Marathon guitar player and ran by St. Louis Cathedral, Linda and Ali were there to cheer us on. Ronnie smiled and waved while they snapped pictures.

"You look great!" they yelled.

"I feel great!" she yelled back, then turned to me. "You know, we really should have signed up for the full marathon. This is a perfect day, the perfect course, it all would have been perfect!"

We laughed and chattered about all we'd seen, about the wharves rising up to our right and the French Quarter's historic buildings passing on our left. Then, with no previous hint of trouble, Ronnie gasped and clutched her stomach.

"Oh wow," she said.

"What's wrong?" I asked.

"Oh wow!" she said louder. A moment ago she was fine. Now her legs were wobbling, she was holding her breath, and her face was contorting. "I think I'm going to get sick."

We were just a few miles from the end, and she was being slammed with one of the most frustrating maladies to affect a runner. Her stomach was in an uproar. I'd been through this sort of thing before. You feel ready to run, you don't want to lose even a step, and yet your innards declare an insurrection, and every step feels like twenty minutes on a Tilt-A-Whirl.

An extra layer of perspiration beaded across her brow, as if typhoid had returned to the river and chosen this moment to strike. She kept gasping, digging her hand into her side, and shaking her head each time I asked, "How are you now?"

There was nothing else I could do. No medicine would help her fast enough even if we had some. A gut-wrenching gallop into the bushes to deposit everything rumbling inside her would help only a bit. So I kept asking the same question every hundred yards as we slowed more and more.

"It's bad," she grunted between teeth clenched in pain, effort, and frustration.

"Hold it together. Just keep moving," I coached. We were almost walking.

We reached 11.5 miles.

Twelve miles.

The distance crawled. The clock raced. The look of dejection on her face was awful. I knew she could go on only if she could master the pain.

Sports lore is filled with advice on exercising while sick: running with a cold, the flu, diarrhea, and malaria; running while vomiting, sneezing, coughing, and experiencing skull-shattering migraines. In short, it might be uncomfortable to run with physical difficulties, but not fatal. I thought perhaps this knowledge would help her, even though it was along the same lines of telling a child to eat his vegetables because someone else, somewhere else, is hungry.

"You know," I said to Ronnie with a grin, "a woman running

the Chicago Marathon went into labor during the race and delivered a baby girl afterward. Isn't that something?"

She looked deeply annoyed. "Your point?"

"She was probably uncomfortable too."

"I'm not just uncomfortable. I feel as if someone is clawing at my insides with a garden tool."

"Yeah, well, I just . . ."

"And if you don't watch it, I'm going to throw up on your shoes."

I lapsed into silence. The heavy breathing of all the other runners filled our ears. I looked at their clean shoes and wondered if I'd be the only victim. Then I had an idea.

"You're fine," I said.

It was a mantra she had heard many times before. From Ronnie's earliest days, Linda and I had always greeted each scraped knee, bruised forehead, or bloody nose with a splash of water and the same words: "You're fine." Linda had purchased a bright red washcloth to clean up childhood wounds so that the girls could not see the blood. We were not being cruel. We believed that one of the most terrifying things for a child is frightened parents. "You're fine." So no matter what kind of calamity befell the girls, we always downplayed it, even if our own hearts were pounding with uncertainty. "You're fine." We'd said it too many times to count.

There was one particularly notable incident when Ronnie was four and fell into a bed of cacti in the Colorado hills. She howled as if she'd been branded. I picked her up to run, crashing through the scrub oaks, back to the car, all the way repeating, "You're fine. You're fine."

At this moment, I hoped the traditional words of comfort

and dismissal would help. "You're fine," I said again. We ran another hundred yards, and she didn't respond.

"You're fine," I said again, as much a prayer as a comment.

Fifty yards more.

"You're fine."

And then it was true. Ronnie took a deep breath. Another. She straightened her back. Just as quickly as the nausea had come, it had gone. A familiar fire came to her eyes. She might yet be beaten in her long quest to master the marathon, but it would not happen this morning.

"I'm good," she declared with a certainty that seemed impossible moments ago. "I am fine. I'm fine. Let's go."

Our strides opened again. The pavement sped up. The sound of the cheering crowd rose ahead in City Park and pulled us on quicker as we swept past others. There were 12.5 miles gone, 13 miles, 13.1. We sprinted across the finish line laughing and hugging.

We caught the shuttle bus back downtown to shower and join Linda and Ali for breakfast. French toast with bananas Foster on top. We picked up some king cakes and headed to the airport to say our good-byes.

"Are you feeling strong?" I asked Ronnie.

"Yes. The best." It seemed wonderfully true. Whatever doubt had gnawed at her in those awful moments had been beaten into retreat. She'd done something that I'd never seen her do before. She had been in trouble during a run, and instead of collapsing into defeat, complaints, and excuses, she had battled her way through. It was a small victory but an important one. The marathon would be filled with challenges like that, and she would have to overcome them all if she wanted to cross that finish line. She hugged us all and said, "Thanks for making this happen." She headed toward her gate, saying over her shoulder, "Best training run ever!"

She jetted off to Atlanta. We went back to D.C.

In the air, I looked out at the Mississippi, coiling through the bayous, farm fields, and old plantation homes, snaking down from Middle America with tankers, barges, and container ships. I thought about their journey to the gulf, and their longer trips out over the oceans and all the lands beyond.

"Only a few more big runs left, and it will be time for the real race," I said to Linda and Ali, who was, as always, grinding away at homework.

I closed my eyes and slept.

NINE

I need sixteen miles."

When I traveled, training was complicated. I not only had to figure out routes in cities I barely knew but also had to fit training in with schedules that might require a hundred hours of work or more a week. During a trip to Las Vegas, we were covering stories about the economy, and everything was behind schedule. Each interview took twice as long as planned. Every place we visited took much longer to reach than we had budgeted. Over and over, we found ourselves forced into the stop-and-go traffic cruising the Strip. And as the day evaporated, I began hating the flashing lights, the gaudy casinos, and the mobs of tourists. I had visited a website for runners in the morning and picked out a wonderful trail in the wilderness, if only I could make it there.

The hours crawled, and by the time we settled in to edit our story in the million-dollar bus called the CNN Express, the day was slipping away.

"I have to get in sixteen miles," I said again to my producer, Katie Ross.

"I heard you. We have to get this done, so keep your shirt on. I mean that, by the way," she said.

She and the crew had already been treated to the unforgettable sight of my winter running gear: black skintight pants, a thermal top, gloves, and a hat. I looked like a cross between Baryshnikov and the Red Hot Chili Peppers. The cameraman, the engineer, the bus driver, and the editor were amused. Katie was not.

She was in her twenties, a decent runner in her own right, and an excellent TV producer who understood the importance of a proper life-work balance, which is not something that can be said about everyone in the news business. She was also of proud Italian descent, with dark hair and black eyes that told anyone in a heartbeat, *"Don't mess me with, or you'll regret it."* With my tendency toward smart-aleck cracks and general dumb-assery, it was a look I was hit with half a dozen times a day.

But she understood what I was trying to accomplish and helped all she could. As soon as we had our script finished and I had recorded my audio track, she dropped the leash. "I've got the story under control. Go!"

I bolted to the rental car and tore off to the west side of Vegas, winding toward a scenic area called Red Rock Canyon. Even as I drove like a bat out of hell, I knew I was pushing my luck with sundown. I just didn't know how far.

The houses fell away, the countryside opened, and in twenty minutes I was pulling up to a magnificent southwestern scene of low desert brush, red rock formations, and rolling hills laced with fossils. The tension of the day was already receding.

"Hi, how much to get into the park?" I asked the gate attendant, a senior citizen wearing a saggy uniform and a ranger's badge. His name tag said Dave.

"Seven dollars, but you don't want to pay that now."

"Why?"

"We're closing in five minutes."

The tension rushed back. My heart sank. I started to pull away, then hesitated.

"Look, I'm a runner. I'm here on business and I just want a place to knock out a few miles. Do you have any suggestions?"

"Oh, sure."

"What?"

"Down the road here about a mile, you'll see a little pull-off. You can leave your car there and run up through the back entrance of the park for free. Only don't stay too long. It'll get dark fast once the sun is gone."

Minutes later, I was running through the stunning valleys and canyons, thanking my lucky stars for Dave's generous advice. Jackrabbits kicked up among the scrub oaks and yuccas. Somewhere hidden in the sparse flora, tortoises crept and wild burros foraged, ground squirrels skittered and bobcats slunk. Cactus wrens, roadrunners, and shrikes worked the blackbrush bushes while a golden eagle soared overhead. The mountains rose sharp and serene, three thousand feet up into the dying day. Streaks of salt and gypsum painted the hills with broad swatches of white and red. Mounds of ghostly Aztec sandstone poked into the air.

The road I was on was smoothly paved and wound around invitingly. There were lots of ups and downs and plenty of scenic turns, and I was soon lost in my thoughts about the people who had traveled this land before me: Paleo-Indians, Ancient Pueblo, and Southern Paiutes to name a few, stretching back over thirteen thousand years. They were hunter-gatherers, but considering the vastness of terrain, there had to be some decent runners among them: men who could chase a wounded deer for hours until it fell or scramble over mountain ranges all day to bring word of a moving herd—or perhaps simply to warn their family and friends that a busload of senior citizens was coming to play Keno. Truth be told, I found it difficult to imagine anyone ever having lived here before modern times if he or she was not committed to the prospect of running on a regular basis.

I remembered a historic account about an extinct southwestern tribe that was so vicious that all the other nearby villages lived in abject terror. This tribe was infamous for virtually every depravity known to man, but one particular tale caught my attention. One appalling day, this crew captured a white trapper who'd strayed into their territory. All indications are that he was a thieving, lying, murdering sort, the kind of shit-kicker Clint Eastwood kills in the first reel in one of his old westerns. Still, the story of what happened to this hapless soul was one for the record books. His hosts, after abusing and defiling him in unimaginable ways, shoved resinous pine splinters into every square inch of his body. Which sounds pretty painful, but that was the good part. The bad part was when they set him on fire.

With neighbors like that, you'd better know how to run.

Everyone who'd ever lived in this area ended up running

somewhere. Of the five Native American groups that roamed what is now the Red Rock Canyon National Conservation Area before settlers came along, none remain. They left a few broken pots and a stone tool or two. Some petroglyphs survive: handprints and indecipherable images incised into the canyon's stones.

Against the sense of deep history and the natural beauty here, the lights of Glitter Gulch seemed far away. Wayne Newton's nightly antics at the Tropicana, the helicopter rides, the escort services, machine-gun ranges, dancing fountains, and exploding pirate ships might as well have been on another planet. For a good hour I felt nothing but the wind, and heard nothing but faint birdcalls and my own steps. I cut off onto side trails as I saw fit. I watched the sky go pink, then purple, then dark blue, then . . .

It happened considerably quicker than I had expected.

One moment I was trotting along thinking that I was due to head back. The next instant, I'd made the turn only to find twilight flooding the valley. The path I'd just run was no longer a warm, seductive strip, but a faint blur of darkness fading into the wilds of Nevada. Night was not falling; it was crashing down. All my reveries about history, geology, and our ancestors vanished like prairie dogs down their holes.

"You should be carrying a phone on your runs," Ronnie had told me a few weeks earlier as I grappled with the cold.

"Why? You think I'm going to be attacked by raccoons?"

"I'm serious. What are you going to do if you get into trouble out there one day?"

"I'll be okay," I'd responded with the bravado of a father.

"She has a point," Linda had added later. "You're covering such distances now, do you realize how hard it would be for me to find you?"

"I don't want the extra weight. A phone slapping against my side the whole time? Come on. That would be miserable."

"Let me tell you, finding your carcass in the weeds by the highway won't be a picnic either. So, will you think about the phone?"

I had sighed. "Sure. I'll think about it."

At this moment, I was wishing I had. I took stock and tried to keep calm. I'd told Katie where I was going in only the vaguest terms. No one knew where I was except Ranger Dave, and I was pretty sure he was home having soup and watching reruns of *The Golden Girls* by now. I'd been running for well over an hour, so I had at least that far to go to reach the car, assuming I made no wrong turns—and in the growing dark, that was hardly guaranteed. Plus, it was getting colder.

I can't count the number of stories I've done over the years about people who set off to hike, picnic, camp, gather wood, or watch birds, only to wind up fighting for their lives at the hands of that cruel harpy, Mother Nature. The West is particularly fertile ground for such tales. The land is filled with sheer cliffs, crumbling escarpments, falling boulders, mine shafts, razor ridges, and mountains so massive that the wrong flank can be as isolated as the dark side of the moon. If you are lucky enough to get lost in a flat section, the advantage is minimal. The landscape is parched in most places, either full-on desert or something close to it. Thornbushes, nettles, cacti, and other vicious plants abound.

The weather is merciless. In the summer, you can be baked

by African heat in the morning, beaten by hailstones the size of toasters at noon, and then buried in six feet of snow by suppertime. Tornadoes, dust storms, wildfires, and hurricane-strength winds are common. On the peaks, lightning pulverizes hikers like a giant bug zapper. In the valleys, flash floods sweep away campers as neatly as a giant toilet.

The only good thing about all that is that it helps you forget the relatively remote possibility of being throttled by a puma, poisoned by a pit viper, gored by a bison, shredded by a bear, or dragged to the ground by fang-baring, slit-eyed coyotes.

The result of all of this is a trail of carnage and despair around those who are unlucky enough to find themselves lost or stranded: elderly couples forced to live weeks on nothing but a box of Cheerios, families stuck in labyrinthine canyons so long that they eat their dogs, college kids buried alive by avalanches, lovers eternally frozen in compromising positions, and at least a few runners who have just disappeared, never to be seen again.

"God, am I stupid," I said. It was a confession, prayer, and question all rolled into one. The longer I ran, the less I seemed to be going anywhere. There was almost no ambient light with which to gauge distance or progress. The road I'd started on, by this time, was nothing but a rumor. I could feel a hard surface beneath my feet, but my steps were blind, and I feared I was on one of the side paths that led to parts unknown. No doubt ancient cartographers would have marked them with words like "Here be dragons!"

I gauged the angle of the asphalt by impact, and guessed where my next step should fall. I knew I could easily miscalculate, break an ankle, and tumble off into a ravine. If I went down out here I would not be found until the next day at the earliest, long after the cold and critters had done their worst.

I could see Ranger Dave shaking his head, surrounded by the search party. *"Dang fool. I told him not to stay too long. Looky there. The varmints done chewed off his shoes!"* I wondered if Wayne Newton would mention me in his show. *"You know, folks, I want to take a moment for a sad song. A song of remembrance . . ."*

I dared not stop. My frantic scramble to get back to the car at that altitude had sapped my energy and drenched my clothes. Every time I backed off, tempted to give in to fatigue, the high desert cold bit into my bones. Even at a dead run, I was shivering and wondering if the operative word would be just that: *dead*. The only thing I could see was the faint glow of Vegas on the horizon far to my left. That bawdy Brigadoon, with its clanging slots, all-you-can-eat buffets, octogenarians toting buckets of nickels, and past-due beauty queens with boobs full of silicone, seemed so lovely now, and I nearly wept at the idea that I might not make it back.

The minutes and miles kept passing. I pushed the button on my watch to trigger the luminous numbers, less to keep track of the time than for the comfort of seeing something that looked like civilization. Then my feet struck metal. I staggered, wobbled, and slipped into a crouch, my feet rolling weirdly. I put a hand down and felt a smooth pole. A cattle crossing.

A car's lights came over the hill so suddenly that I was blinded, then they swerved and swept away. I was right next to a highway. I looked back and forth in the blackness. Another car came in the other direction, and in its lights I saw my own vehicle not more than fifty feet away.

I have rarely enjoyed starting an automobile so much—the purr of the engine, the lights on the dash. I imagined this was the way an astronaut, deep-sea diver, or terrorist hostage might feel upon returning from a doomed journey. I turned the heat and radio up high and rode back into Vegas, singing along with every song, glorying in every sight and sound.

"Where the hell have you been?" Katie yelled the moment I stepped back into the bus. "I thought we were going to have to call out a posse for you."

"Yeah," I said. "Me too."

"That's it," Linda said when I contacted her from my room. She'd been frantically trading calls with Katie during my lost hours. "From now on you are taking a phone."

Having survived, I was cocky. "Look, I really don't have a good place to carry a phone."

"I have one in mind."

She had a point, but I would have to consider it down the line. After all the miles, all the pushing, all the effort, Atlanta was closing in fast. I called Ronnie from D.C. a couple of weeks later.

"Are you ready?" I asked.

"Yep. Are you?"

"I'm getting on the plane. It's time, buddy."

TEN

From our hotel window high up in the darkness, we saw the streets filled in all directions with human ants, churning, seething, scattering in waves. The lights of Centennial Olympic Park flickered against plastic banners flapping in an early breeze. The roar of sixteen thousand runners mixed with a storm front of music pushing through the walls and driving our heart rates up. Down in the lobby, Ronnie and I waded through a chaos of human anxiety. Stepping onto the street, we were enveloped by a straining, surging, lunging herd of shivering suburbanites in nylon shorts. A few weeks after New Orleans, we were ready to battle the great race for which we had trained all this time: the Publix Georgia Marathon. First, however, we had to conquer the crowd. The New Orleans race was large. This was massive.

Working our way to our starting corral through the dense pack on Marietta Street was going to take a while. "Here we are," I said repeatedly, only to have Ronnie shake her head. "No. Not yet. We're farther back."

One of the bigger changes in the world of marathoning is the need for crowd control. Back when few brave souls ventured out for these challenging races, it was easy to give a number to whoever wanted one, jam people up to the starting line, and fire the gun. As the races evolved into bigger spectacles with the attendant dangers of injurious if not life-threatening stampedes, race directors realized the free-for-alls needed refinement. These days the largest races "seed" runners according to their expected finish time. The reasoning is sound. Many fast runners, if trapped behind thousands of casual runners, would morph into maniacs, bobbing, weaving, pushing, and cursing their way to find daylight amid fears of atrocious finish times. Slower runners, in turn, would be forced to endure all the elbows and swearing that come with being in the path of a speed-crazy pack. So when you sign up for a big race these days, you are asked to guess when you might cross the line to collect your medal. Some races even require entrants to show proof of their expected speed by supplying a previous race result.

That is not as draconian as it sounds, because while strong runners are masochistically honest about their successes and failures, many relatively weak runners are inveterate liars, exaggerating their training mileage, deflating their splits, and wildly overestimating their strengths.

"Say, Chuck, how is the marathon training going?"

"I logged a solid sixty miles of training last week. All of it uphill, by the way."

"Really? That must have been tough."

"Piece of cake. And I feel great!"

"Fantastic! What sort of speed were you doing?"

"Oh, I don't track my time. I'm a purist that way. But now that you ask, I was on a seven-minute pace for most of it."

"Seven-minute miles all that way?"

"No. I ran a couple of six-thirties."

Their hole of deception gets deeper when races roll around. Having lied to their running friends, they can't very well just reveal their dishonesty when they fill out an entry form. So these boasters predict finish times they couldn't match if strapped to Danica Patrick's hood. They rationalize. *"I'm running well. When I get excited, I run faster. The race will be exciting. Therefore I'd better put myself down for a 3:00 finish, because you never know."*

You can spot them near the start line, stretching ostentatiously among the elite runners, trying to hide their new shoes and obviously in the grips of rising panic as they notice that every other runner nearby looks like a greyhound on steroids. More experienced runners know it is better to start in a group that is too slow rather than in one that is too fast. I had explained this to Ronnie when we entered the race.

"It's better to start in a corral that is slower than your anticipated time than in one that is even slightly faster."

"Why?" she asked. "Wouldn't we be better off in a group where no one will slow us down?"

"Believe me, no one will slow us down. People get so cranked at the start of these races that they take off like bottle rockets. If we start with a slower group, we can build confidence by passing people for much of the race. If we start with a faster group, we'll be passed most of the time. Which do you think sounds better?"

"I get your point."

"Never try to impress people with where you start. Impress them with where you finish."

My argument also had technology on its side. Long ago, even average runners had to push and shove for good positions since every second lost reaching the starting line was lost forever. The master clock timed everyone equally, and if you took forty-five seconds or five minutes to reach the start through a crowded field, that was just too bad for you. Now most races issue electronic tags, which runners wear on their shoes or connected to their race bibs. When those tags pass over special mats on the course, computers record that runner's time to a split second. That not only eliminates arguments about mistakes by race officials but also cuts down on cheating. After all, you can't very well claim you ran the whole race if three computer checkpoints have no record of you passing their way.

So Ronnie and I had played it safe. We gave ourselves a generous pad of time in which to run her first marathon, and that meant our corral was some distance from the start line. Quite some distance.

"I can't even see the starting line from here," Ronnie said.

"We'll be okay," I said, but I didn't like the look of it either.

I was not reassured when we heard the distant sound of the official start moments later and noticed that our group did not move. After all our preparations and anticipation, it felt as if we were starting with a whimper rather than a bang. We were so deeply buried in the back that we might as well have been spectators. Other runners made nervous jokes and slapped their hands together for warmth. A few hollered, "Let's go!" And after endless minutes, the river of runners oozed forward. At first we walked, then we walked faster, and finally, as the pack opened up enough for us to bend our knees, the mass began bobbing up and down like tribal dancers in the pre-dawn. The start banner, which ended up being a full half mile from our starting corral, swept toward us as huge speakers boomed Journey's "Don't Stop Believin'" into the darkness; it was a hundred feet away, then twenty, then overhead. We stepped across the line, and all our fears of a slow start were swept away in a flash flood of runners.

"Here we go!" Ronnie shouted. A roar answered as our wave rushed down the course. Elbows, knees, feet, and hands boiled on all sides. Police lights flickered through the crowd, the music ricocheted off the buildings. The noise was tremendous. The excitement infectious.

"Easy, easy!" I called to her as the current threatened to carry us into a sprint between twin rows of cheering spectators pushed against the steel barricades. Cardboard signs flapped. Whistles shrieked and cowbells clanged. The pavement was a gray blur. The pack crashed through the rapids of the first quarter mile and turned a corner, and the din of the starting area faded. As if coming up for air, everyone took a breath. Small gaps appeared as runners spread out across the road, slowed, and collected themselves.

Ronnie turned to me and laughed. "Wow! That was crazy."

"Yes, it was," I said. "Now let's settle down and run our race."

We'd chosen our corral wisely. We spent the first mile passing slower runners, skipping onto the sidewalk around tight knots of folks, and chatting about the dawn just beginning to color the sky. We cruised above I-85 on an overpass, and I said, "Hey, here is something that will be fun. When we come back across this highway later in the race, I want you to say, 'I do declare we've passed this way before!'" I affected my best Rhett Butler accent, and she chuckled.

"Okay. I've got it. When will we pass over it again?"

"In about twenty miles."

It was a silly joke, but breaking down the marathon's fearsome distance into smaller moments and landmarks is a time-tested way of keeping up a newbie's enthusiasm. So is keeping a sense of humor.

Despite my twenty-year absence from the race, I was undaunted. First, because I felt prepared. Second, because I was much more interested in pacing Ronnie than I was in my own finishing time.

Atlanta, like many marathon–half marathon combinations, begins with everyone running together. Three out of every four runners are there for the shorter distance, which creates an odd rhythm for novices. This was why I guarded so carefully against us exploding out of the gate. Getting caught up in an early rush can make completing 13.1 miles uncomfortable, but the same premature need for speed can turn 26.2 miles into agony. I knew that I needed to keep Ronnie moving fast enough to enjoy a solid race but slow enough to finish without an ambulance.

And then there were the hills.

Some weeks earlier, I had looked up the elevation chart. In most races, this is a tidy little graph showing lots of flat sections, a half-dozen mild bumps, and perhaps three or four sharper climbs of fifty or a hundred feet. The Atlanta chart was such a wicked line of peaks and valleys I assumed at first that it must be somehow out of scale. I'd never noticed hills in my previous visits to the city, and if you told anyone you were running a long race there, they would likely suspect a gently rolling course at worst. And yet there the hills were, like the jagged teeth of an alligator. As we approached the three-mile mark, the jaws closed around.

"*Oof*," Ronnie said, leaning up the slope and digging in. "I didn't see this coming."

"What do you mean?" I asked. "You train here all the time."

"Yeah, *here* as in 'in this city,' but not *here* as in 'right here.' This is tough."

It grew tougher. The Atlanta course is well designed. It passes through several institutes of higher learning: Georgia State University, Agnes Scott College, Emory University, and Georgia Tech. It passes the Jimmy Carter Presidential Library and Museum. Carter used to sneak out of the Oval Office for daily runs with a small security detail. I once asked him if he was ever spotted by tourists. He flashed that famous grin and said, "Sometimes, but they could never catch me." The course also goes by the birthplace and burial site of Martin Luther King, Jr. As we wound through the beautiful, tree-lined neighborhoods that make Atlanta such a lovely town, the trail seemed to find every bump or incline.

By the time we split off from the halfers, we were feeling it, and so was everyone else. A guy named Raphael fell in next to us. He was from Peru, and while we all agreed that the weather was nice for this run, the hills were another matter.

"Considering where you are from, I guess these are no big deal to you," I said.

"Oh, no," he said. "They're a big deal. I didn't expect this at all."

"Me neither. I looked at the elevation chart but . . ."

"But you didn't believe it! Me neither. I figured it just couldn't be that bad."

I nodded at Ronnie, who was chugging away beside us.

"It's her first marathon."

Raphael grinned weakly. "Congratulations. You picked a hell of a race to start with."

As if on cue, we ran past a stand of trees and saw the steepest hill yet ahead. A groan rose from the field in a preview of what we would experience repeatedly for the next few hours.

"Do these things ever end?" Raphael asked.

"Yeah," Ronnie said. "At the finish line."

We put our heads down and powered to the top. There were bright spots, which were mercifully flat, like the wonderful pass through the suburb of Decatur, where fans lined the streets and cheered as if we were chasing a world record. Every runner around us relaxed, shook off some of the weariness, and started smiling again. Even a Mylar balloon that drifted into a power line and then exploded as loudly as a cannon caused nothing more than nervous laughter and shouts of excitement.

The smiles fell away when we hit the neighborhood called, appropriately, Druid Hills. I was monitoring Ronnie's progress and noticed she was shortening her stride more than I'd expected. We had cracked seventeen miles, and were facing yet another steep climb, when she stopped cold, bending over until her fingertips touched her shoes.

"What's wrong? Your stomach? Your back? Your knees?" My questions flew. She stood up, her eyes searching and hurting.

"It's my butt. The muscles are killing me."

The dreaded butt cramps.

One feature of human beings that makes us better than any other creature on earth at long-distance running is our large butt muscles. Other muscles may appear more elegant, but the gluteus truly is maximus. These twin outboard engines of muscle play a magnificent role in snapping our legs back and forth mile after mile. Evolution has left gorillas, chimps, and orangutans with a lot of our DNA, and they use less energy than we do when they run. But think about how they look: arms flailing over their heads, hips swinging side to side, toes twisted inward. That's because while our simian cousins have some of our assets, they don't have our asses. That's why we can run long and hard, and they can't.

I once heard about a man in Australia who had an entire cheek bitten off by a rogue camel. Although he survived, I have forever imagined him running wide circles in the outback, deprived of the balancing power of his second buttock. The butt is so critical that if you literally ran your ass off, it would be the last running you ever did. Accordingly, when a human develops a pain in the ass during a marathon, it's a problem.

In the time-honored tradition of men who don't know what else to do, I urged Ronnie, "Stretch it out. Keep walking," which she'd heard from me many times before in her life. Fall from a tree, hitting every branch on the way down? Walk it off. Get thrown from the back of a mad sheep at the neighborhood rodeo? Walk it off. Struck by a meteorite? Walk it off. Had Ali been on hand, the sarcasm would have been thicker than the humidity over Ronnie's misery and my insufferable advice. Instead, Ronnie said nothing, and we hobbled up the road. She was panting hard, I was looking at my watch, and we were both considering our options.

Quitting was not one of them. Sure, she was in agony, but that was fleeting. I thought of how my first marathon ended in ignominious, limping defeat at mile 21, and knew how a Did Not Finish would haunt her. I also remembered a sign we'd seen a spectator holding miles before: "Pain is temporary. Times posted on the Internet are forever."

The problem was twofold. She was not taking in enough liquids, and she was losing too much salt through her sweat. That one-two punch is the primary reason cramps appear. I spotted an aid station ahead and formulated an instant plan, which I barked like gospel. "You need to drink more. Grab some Powerade. Grab some water. Grab some more! More!"

She drained the little paper cups. I reached into a small pocket on the back of my shorts and pulled out two tiny, bright bits.

"Now eat these!" I said.

"What are they?"

And without a hint of a smile, I said, "They are magic beans."

For my money, they really were. Some weeks earlier, I'd gone out for a long training run on a weekend. The twenty miles of hills and canal path were brutal. Despite gulping water and maintaining a reasonable pace, I was staggering by mile 17, just as Ronnie was now. My thighs, calves, and buttocks were drained, cramping, and threatening to shut down. My shoulders were slumping. My head was aching. My stomach was a mess.

That afternoon I scoured the Internet for clues as to what had gone wrong and came across a simple explanation. I'd let my salts and sugars get out of balance. I needed a supplement. The answer, which I found that evening at a sports store, was beans.

Not normal beans, but specially formulated jelly beans that pack in each sugary, explosive bite a load of the very things that pour out of your body when you sweat. The next weekend I gave them a try. At mile 9, as my legs started dragging, I chewed two of them. The change was instantaneous and miraculous, as if someone had poured pure energy into my muscles. Not crazy, amphetamine-like "Hey, kids, let's swim the English Channel!" energy, but instead smooth, velvety power. Fatigue faded. My spirit and stride sharpened. The effect lasted about three miles, then I popped some more beans, and I was good to go. When I pulled up to my house after twenty-two miles of running, I felt fantastic. I went inside crowing about the miracles of modern nutrition to Linda, who smiled politely, said she was glad, and then told me to take out the trash.

I watched for Ronnie's reaction with great anticipation, and sure enough, within a minute she was moving much more steadily, the pain falling from her face.

"Better?" I asked.

"Much. What's in those things?"

"Sugar. Salt. Everything you need."

I had made Ronnie violate a cardinal rule of marathoning: Never try anything on race day that you haven't tried first in training. Those fancy new shoes hide stiff parts that will rub your feet raw. That power bar your friend told you to scarf down might be great for him but may scrub your intestines like steel wool. Even that cute pair of 26.2 socks you loved at the race expo can work up blisters so fast you'll be hating them by mile 10.

But desperate times require desperate measures, and I knew enough about Ronnie's past struggles with distance running and her constitution to take a chance. And it kept working. She was still hurting, and we stopped periodically so that she could stretch, but the sharpest pain was subsiding, and her suffering was taking on the normal shape that all beginning marathoners know and love.

"Can we walk a little here?" she asked as we faced another hill at mile 19.

"We can, but you should know something. This is where you will win or lose your race."

"I'm not going to win the race."

"I said 'your race.' I know that you'd like to finish in less than five hours today, and you are on pace, but if you fall off here, you'll never make it up in the later miles. It's too hard."

She considered that for a moment. "Give me some beans."

All things considered, she was running brilliantly. Marathoning is as much about adjusting expectations as it is about raw effort. A smart, committed runner can make it through the miles even when he is not feeling great purely by managing his muscles, his resources, and his mind. She was doing all three. Her butt had been hurting, so she was easing up on the hills to give it a break. Her system was teetering, so she was loading up on liquids. Her head was fogged by fatigue, but her central thought remained clear and directed: Get to the end.

Although, to be fair, I had created an addict.

"Beans!"

I usually took beans every thirty minutes. She started hitting them every mile. "Beans!" she said as we roared into Piedmont Park shortly after mile 21. "Beans!" she said again as we headed toward an awkward reverse turn, sweeping past many of the other runners we'd been tracking all day.

"Raphael!" we called out when we spotted our Peruvian friend. He'd made the corner and was coming back past us. "You're looking good!"

He beamed. "You too! Keep going!"

"Beans!" Ronnie cried.

I had a fleeting image of her winding up hopelessly hooked—living in a shelter, running all day, hanging out near sports stores panhandling beans to keep herself going. I'd have no one to blame but myself. Dad. Bean pusher. I popped a couple myself, and within seconds I was feeling better.

Everyone was.

Something magical happens in the last four miles of a marathon. You would think it would happen at twenty miles, but at that point there is still enough distance ahead to keep spirits in check. After twenty-two, however, everyone smells the finish line. Eyes that have been glued to the next piece of pavement are raised to the horizon. Feet that are shuffling start stepping. Like trail horses at a dude ranch, everyone can sense the barn, and most start running again. Not fast, but running nonetheless.

It happened for Ronnie as we passed a woman holding a sign with the universal battle cry of Georgia Tech: "Go Yellow Jackets." Ronnie grinned for the first time in two hours.

We shot past our favorite Waffle House and hit the interstate overpass. Ronnie turned to me with a sly grin on her sweat-streaked face. "I do declare we've passed this way before!" she said. We were both still laughing when we rumbled onto the Georgia Tech campus and raced past her dorm. The worst of the hills, the aching, the cramps, the blisters, and the doubts were behind us. There were some tough miles ahead, but the math was clear. The finish line was no longer abstract. It was real and just out of sight. We passed mile 23. All those weeks of training were coming down to little more than another half hour of running. It was fun again.

A guy on the sidewalk with a computer bag called out, "Hey, Ronnie, good run! Keep going!"

"Oh no," she said as we raced out of earshot. "That guy is in one of my classes, and my hair looks awful!"

We laughed again. Up Tech Parkway she chirped once more, "Beans!"

I dug into my pocket. "That's the last of them. We're at mile 25, and you'll have to tough it out from here."

"I can do it," she said.

Some spectators had set up loudspeakers that were blasting Stevie Wonder's "Isn't She Lovely." I looked at my daughter bounding along beside me and thought, yes she is. She really is. As much advice as I'd given her since the start, she probably thought I'd coached her through this feat with my words of encouragement, my runner's wisdom, and my beans, but I knew better. In the end, like every runner who succeeds at the marathon, she'd mastered it on her own. There is no other way. What's more, although I had given up on ever doing anything like this again, she'd pulled me like Lazarus back from the Tomb of Lost Runners. Then, 26.2 glorious miles after we started, we heard the roaring crowd, and we cruised across the line in Centennial Olympic Park, father and daughter united in the wonder of a wish fulfilled.

"Come here," she said in the milling post-race throng. "Take off your medal."

"Why?" I asked.

"Just do it."

I lifted the ribbon from my neck, the glittering medal swinging, She did the same but immediately reached up to put her medal over my head, presenting it to me. "I'm giving you my medal," she said, "because without you on my team, I never would have accomplished this. I know we each had to run alone a lot, but I felt like you were with me every step of the way. No one was left behind."

I hugged her and gave her my medal in return.

"Are you going to wear that on the plane?" I asked.

"Yeah. You should too," she said. "We earned them. And how many days in your life can you say that?"

Ronnie was right. She was flying with me back to D.C. to start her spring break, and we boarded like Olympians. When we landed, Linda and Ali cheered as if we were world record holders. They had a decorated cake and tiny trophies waiting for us. It was a triumph for Ronnie, and it was for me too. Finally, for the first time, I had truly trained to be a runner, and the results were wonderful.

As I look back, that's probably where the madness began.

ELEVEN

My mother was wary of the whole running enterprise. She was just past her eightieth birthday and came from a generation in which normal people rarely ran, unless they were being chased. After the race, she was relieved and congratulated both of us. My sister, Chris, older than I am by six years, was similarly supportive, as she has been of practically every endeavor in my life. If I had a dollar for every time she endured my walking into a room as a child and saying, "I have a magic trick to show you!" I'd be richer than Bill Gates.

My brother, Robert, older by three years, was the one I was worried about. He owns a small construction company in L.A., meaning Lower Alabama, where he puts roofs onto homes, renovates kitchens, raises barns, and occasionally builds houses. His labor is hard, his handiwork is excellent, and he is as tough as a human being can be. Our relationship has always been competitive, even though his superior height, weight, and athleticism have allowed him to crush me since birth in pretty much any contest. This did not keep me from taking up his challenges, however, and grabbing victories where I could. None of which was ever well received.

One blazing summer day when I was twelve, and we lived amid the soybean fields of Illinois, we were boxing on the concrete slab in front of the garage. We were wearing tattered leather gloves my dad had rescued from the trash bin of a military gym when he was in the Air Force, and Robert was slapping me stupid as usual. I was enduring the abuse in exchange for the remote chance of landing a stray punch. Then he did the unforgivable.

"Hold on a second, Tom," he said, dripping with condescension. "Let me teach you something about boxing."

Those were fighting words. I had watched many more boxing matches on TV than he ever had. I had listened to post-fight analyses much more closely. I had clipped pictures of Muhammad Ali, Joe Frazier, and George Foreman out of the newspaper and taped them to my closet door. In a shallow, media-fed way, I felt I was much more closely tied to that Holy Trinity of ring greatness than Robert would ever be.

"What are you going to do?" I fired back. "Teach me to be a foot taller? Teach me to have longer arms?"

He chuckled as if I were a furious four-year-old. "You just have to learn to protect yourself," he said. "Now, punch me in the stomach."

I knew what he meant: *Pretend to hit me in the stomach in slow motion so I can display my superior understanding of the sport. I will clamp my elbows together to block your punch, and your comprehension of boxing will be expanded, thanks to my generous sharing of my Solomon-like wisdom.*

I also knew what he'd actually said. I threw the hardest, quickest jab of my soon-to-be-over amateur boxing career: a penetrating punch backed up by all of my 130 pounds, driving the air from his lungs and surprise into his face. His eyes bugged. His knees buckled. His arms fell limp. For a tenth of a second. Then he roared up to his full height, drew his gloves back, and wailed on me. To this day I don't know how many times he hit me as I scrambled to escape, only that he finished with a rousing series of Ken Norton overhands that drove me into the ground like a nail.

It was worth every second.

Against his undeniable superiority in almost all sports, it is a wonder I tried to compete. When we'd marathoned together all those years ago, he was gracious and encouraging, mainly because, although I could beat him in many long runs, he was able to edge me out in those gargantuan races through a lot more training and pure big-brother bullheadedness.

I was curious, however, how he would respond to my latest attempts. He had returned to distance running himself a few months earlier in the Pensacola Marathon. He enjoyed it, but the times posted by Ronnie and me were about a half hour faster than his. In addition, just six days after the Atlanta race, Ronnie had suggested that we hop into the National Half Marathon in Washington, D.C. Despite a cold day, and our throbbing legs, we finished in fine form, pushing our racing mileage for the week to 39.3 miles. Add the shakedown runs we'd done in between races, and we were at well over forty-five miles. Ronnie understood her uncle's competitive streak and questioned when and how I would tell him about all this.

"He might not be happy," she'd said.

"Uncle Robert and I are in our fifties, sweetie. We're not little kids anymore competing for attention."

"But you're still brothers. You know how that can be."

I stepped into the minefield gingerly with a call shortly after the D.C. half. His response made me instantly ashamed of our doubts. "That's great! That is outstanding!" The unchained warmth coming through the phone from Alabama was enough to make all the training worth it. "You must really be doing some excellent running. I'm so proud of you, and Ronnie too. Tell me all about it."

"The marathon was a blast and the half was pretty good. Freezing, but fun."

"I'll bet. I would have loved running with you."

"Maybe we should try it next year."

"You know what I'm thinking?" he said. "The New Orleans half sounded like a great run. Let's meet down there next winter, and we'll do the full marathon together."

"It's certainly flat enough to make it fun."

"Even better! We can stop for muffulettas at the halfway mark!"

His encouragement meant more than a hundred medals. Despite all those years of duking it out in sports, here he was glowing about his little brother outrunning him, and it made us closer than racing together ever had. My father had passed away from cancer a few years earlier, uniting us in sorrow, and this seemed like the next natural step in our burgeoning relationship.

Robert and I spoke almost every Sunday afternoon from that day on, and running dominated. We rattled on about mileage, shoes, what pain relievers were best, and what training programs were worst. We discussed races in the past and races in the future. When I decided to run the inaugural

Gettysburg Marathon, only a month and a half after Atlanta, he was solidly in my corner.

"You've done the training. Sounds like you're running well. Go for it, buddy."

Linda remained at the intersection of enthusiastic and reserved. She found this whole running craze entertaining, and had backed my efforts with Ronnie from the beginning. Now, however, she suspected something daffy was developing.

"How long do you intend to keep doing this?" she asked the day before the Gettysburg race. We had driven to Pennsylvania to pick up my race packet and were cruising the course. "Aren't you supposed to take some time off after running a marathon?"

"I've heard that," I said.

"How much?"

"Some people say you should rest one day for every mile in the race."

"So you shouldn't have run even once in the past month."

"The past month and a half if you count the D.C. race."

"And you rested how many days?"

"Three. Well, two."

She sighed and we continued to ride the race route. It soared up and down mountains, around orchards, past barns, through valleys, and beside streams. After twenty miles, we rounded yet another corner to see yet another hill, and she summed up her thoughts. "You're doomed."

She was nearly right. Rising the next morning in the dark, I dawdled grabbing breakfast and missed the start. By the time I'd parked and caught the shuttle bus over, the other runners were gone, spectators were milling, and the clock said three minutes had elapsed since the gun. I sprinted across the line and went belting up the road, a runner in search of a race.

Before the first two miles were done, I'd found it, and it was magnificent. My late launch proved a godsend. Gone was all the typical pressure of an early start. With no one else around, I was running my own race from the first step, and by the time I caught up with the pack, I had settled into a comfortable rhythm. I ran happily and easily. Midway I was picking up speed, running the first negative splits in my personal marathoning history, which is to say I was on track to run the second half of the race faster than the first half. I talked with other runners and made jokes. I drank in the scenery and enjoyed the beautiful weather. I felt no fatigue as I eased along at a pace that felt as comfortable as a walk around the block. Blasting across the finish line in a time of 4:21, a full twenty-five minutes faster than in Atlanta, I grabbed my medal and a bottle of water and headed home feeling nearly as fresh as when I'd started.

I called Ronnie as I drove. "Oh man, I can't believe your time," she said. "I thought we did well in Atlanta. How'd you finish so fast?"

"I just felt good," I said. "And I've kept running. How about you? I missed you out there."

"My training hasn't been so great. Honestly, my aerospace classes are beating me senseless, and I'm hardly running at all."

"That's okay. Sometimes it's just too hard to fit everything in. You've got to work out a balance."

"You know, I have a secret to tell you."

"What's that?"

"I missed a training run. You know that twenty-two-miler on that Sunday a couple of weeks before the race? I had to go to a big meeting with my scholarship group, and I couldn't make it work. There just wasn't enough time."

"That's okay. You finished the race anyway, didn't you?"

"But I broke one of our rules."

"You know, Ronnie," I said, "I understand why that troubles you. I've always been a rule follower at heart, and one of the things I've learned is that sometimes rules have to be broken. I never much like doing it, but I always tell myself that we have to run each day for tomorrow."

"What does that mean?"

"What happens with today's run doesn't matter if it makes you unable or unwilling to run tomorrow. The long run is the goal. So if you miss a run, or a week of running, or even six months, you can't let it tear you down so much that you give up on the idea of trying. You may miss a run now and then, but you're a real runner now, sweetie. You're a marathoner. Don't forget that."

We gabbed a bit more, and I sensed that closeness I'd been hoping for in the backwash of the Atlanta race. As I drove home, the sun through the windshield was warm, and the traffic was light. Linda and I went out for a late lunch. She patiently endured my play-by-play of the race with a tiny smile flitting across her face. I asked her what was so funny. She said, "I think I know you. Aren't you that guy who used to run up and down the roadside hoping I'd drive by?" We laughed. Later, I napped off some of the fatigue on the sofa, and that evening the phone rang.

"Hey, bro. How'd it go?"

It was Robert calling for an update. I walked him through the race, told him about some of the other runners I'd met, and described the medal. We analyzed the highs and lows. Then, just as I was about to say good-bye, light a fire, and settle in to watch some hockey, he raised a question I hadn't considered. In retrospect, I don't know why it seemed so unexpected, but at that moment, it flashed like the proverbial lightbulb in my head, illuminating a previously unseen landscape of possibilities.

"So," Robert said, "you've done all this work. What's next?"

TWELVE

Completing the Atlanta marathon had been the only goal. Everything afterward had been icing on the cake. I had picked up those other races because there was no good reason not to. After all my years of slacking, I was pleased to prove I could still mow down the miles. I was enjoying myself, and the idea of extending the experience was attractive. Having dug myself up from the depths of middle-aged sloth, I realized I was craving a new goal, something more ambitious than just bagging more races. But, as Robert had asked, what?

A conversation started by Wolf Blitzer led to the answer.

At work, I'd become part of the circle of men and women who are running journalists. When we'd encounter one another in the halls or on assignments, we'd invariably talk about our latest training sessions and what races we were considering. As one of these extemporaneous meetings of the CNN running club was breaking up, Wolf passed on the way to the studio.

Wolf is a wonderful man, generous and professional. He always has a good word for any and all colleagues, and he keeps up with our varied interests as if they were Middle East peace negotiations. He also has an endearing and amusing tendency to greet nearly everyone by his or her full name.

"What are you talking about, Tom Foreman?" Wolf said.

"Running. You run pretty often, don't you, Wolf?"

"Five miles a day on the treadmill."

"We should go running together."

"How far do you run?"

"I've done two marathons and two half marathons so far this year."

"This year?"

"This year."

"You're a wild man, Tom Foreman."

And he was gone. In the middle of this conversation, another coworker had strolled up. I knew my fellow correspondent Lisa Sylvester was a good runner. How good, I had no idea.

"You know what you should do?" she said. "With all that training you have under your belt, you should consider an ultramarathon."

"Hmm. I don't think so." I'd heard rumors of such things and assumed they were largely mythical, existing only in the rarified air of super athletes, if at all, but Lisa persisted.

"Oh, they're great fun," she said. "I ran the JFK 50 some years ago and had a really good time."

"What does the '50' stand for?"

"Miles. It's a fifty-mile race started by President Kennedy."

"So, is this spread out over a couple of days?"

"No. It's all at once," she said.

My brow furrowed as if she were proposing a snipe hunt.

"I don't think I could do that," I said.

"Sure you could," she said. "And if not that one, you should try another. They're all over the place."

One of the truisms I have learned through more than three decades of reporting is that good ideas are easily killed, but bad ideas hang around like vampires surviving virtually every attempt to knock them off. Such was the case with this one.

I googled "ultrarunning" and found that Lisa was not kidding. There was a whole world of people out there running far beyond the limits of the marathon and/or common sense. Races of 50, 60, and 75 miles. A fair number of these intrepid souls race 100 miles or more in dreadful conditions: at high altitudes, in scorching heat, in brutal cold, in deserts, and through godforsaken wilderness. To say that this was a revelation is an understatement, in the same sense that it would be a revelation to find out that my dog could talk.

At the lowest level are the 50-kilometer races. Just over 30 miles, these are basically overgrown marathons, and plenty of top-flight marathoners cover that distance in the course of a regular race if you include their warm-ups and cool-downs. Many ultrarunners think of 50K races as pleasure cruises. They'll jump into one with no special preparation, knock it out before the sun is high, and be back home grilling burgers by lunchtime, none the worse for the wear.

They get serious only when the big boys show up: the 50-milers.

As Lisa mentioned, these races can be found in every state, lurking in forests, along rivers, through deserts, and atop mountain ridges—anyplace a series of roads and trails can be patched together to form a full route of 50 miles or more. Many are defined as much by their dangers as by their distance. Some are known for their ankle-breaking rocks, others for their shoe-stealing mud, and still others for their lung-smothering dust. There are plenty of odd distances, and, frankly, a good bit of odd behavior. Some races stipulate that runners must carry everything with them, while others have plentiful aid stations. Some are repeated loops around well-marked paths, while others are little more than bushwhacked rumors of routes through unforgiving wastelands.

And then the even bigger boys come calling. Badwater is a 135-mile race that starts in the scorching heat of Death Valley and climbs more than 8,000 feet to the finish. The Western States Endurance Run rumbles up and down the steep hills of the Sierra Nevada for 100 miles. The Hardrock 100 does the same in the Rockies.

Of course, the United States doesn't hold all the honors.

In Canada, the Yukon Arctic Ultra is a whole different level of extreme. There, runners are offered a choice of distances in which to compete up to and including 470 miles. They must pull all their provisions in sleds while keeping an eye out for wolves, wolverines, irritable moose, and temperatures known to drop to 40 below zero. For all this mind-blowing endurance and derring-do, they earn a T-shirt and a certificate.

Congratulations. Should we just toss these frozen toes, or should we box them up so you can take them home with you?

For those who dislike frostbite, the Sahara Desert offers a similar race in which competitors carry their supplies while stumbling up, over, and down sand dunes for six days in the Marathon des Sables. Granted, there are no bears or wolves, but life in a natural frying pan playing the part of human bacon is no doubt challenging enough.

Even tiny Wales boasts a 186-mile, five-day run down its mountainous spine called Ras Cefn y Ddraig (Dragon's Back Race). The website warns that the race between two castles is on "wild, remote, and totally trackless ground." Oh, how the Welsh love a good understatement. Competitors carry maps and compasses to navigate up gut-wrenching pitches and down death-defying slopes, while dodging rainstorms, car-size boulders, and undoubtedly biblical bouts of ennui. Just watching video of this race can make strong men weep uncontrollably.

Other races have names so horrific that extended descriptions are hardly needed, including La Diagonale des Fous (the Madmen's Diagonal); the Jungle Marathon, complete with waist-deep muck and 99 percent humidity; the Spartathlon, in Pheidippides' old hood; Tor de Géants (Tour of Giants); and La Ultra, in which Himalayan altitudes add the exquisite possibility of your brain exploding to the list of potentially fatal threats.

Each of these races is touted as the most difficult on earth, and I suspect that might be true for any one of them, considering how they routinely produce photos of competitors collapsed on the ground, staring catatonically and peeling the skin off their feet like socks. It's no surprise, then, that most ultramarathons draw relatively few runners. The smallest may involve a dozen competitors, and even a robust ultra may pull only a few hundred.

The exception is the most renowned and largest ultramarathon on the planet, Comrades. Centered in the hills outside Durban, South Africa, it began back in 1921 as a tribute to soldiers who died in World War I. Comrades draws some

20,000 runners, or slightly less than one-third of the total number of people to compete in ultramarathons each year. Some years the course starts in the mountains and runs down to the town. Other years it starts in the town and runs up to the mountains. Either way, runners have twelve hours to complete fifty-six miles, and if they fall short by even a minute, they'll find themselves dismissed as if they did not run at all.

"Have you ever heard of these races?" I asked Ronnie on the phone.

"Can't say I have," she replied. "Kind of hard to believe they actually exist. Sounds like Bigfoot."

"Hey, Bigfoot is real, and I won't have you mocking him."

"Anyway, are you seriously considering this?"

"No. Yes. Maybe. I don't know."

"Sounds like a plan to me. And if you do enter one, make sure Mom takes out more insurance on you, okay? I want to finish college."

Her Bigfoot comparison was apt. The idea that these runners were living among us made me imagine legions of them in the suburban woods, emerging at dusk, sprinting through the trees, communicating with hoot owl sounds, and melting into the gloom as soon as an outsider ventured near.

Quietly, so as not to excite unwanted scrutiny from coworkers who already thought I might be going balmy, I started buying and borrowing books on the subject of ultrarunning. I cruised race websites checking on sign-up dates, locations, and courses, and gradually I found myself circling around to the race Lisa had first mentioned.

The JFK 50 is the oldest and most famous ultramarathon in the United States. The course is situated north of D.C. It starts with some steep up-and-down rambling among the pointy rocks and tight paths of the Appalachian Trail, then transitions into a long slog on a section of the canal path on which I train, and finally follows some winding country roads to the finish line. Like a lot of venerable institutions, it comes with a good story, which, oddly enough, doesn't begin with John Fitzgerald Kennedy. It does, however, involve a president. In 1908, the Oval Office was held by that enthusiastic outdoorsman and fitness fanatic Theodore Roosevelt. Ever since overcoming chronic illness in his youth, Teddy had dived into every physical challenge imaginable with the greatest gusto. Scaling the Matterhorn? No problem. Hunting buffalo with a pocketknife? Piece of cake. Boxing with his cabinet members like Gentleman Jim Corbett hopped up on schnapps? Bully!

The Athlete in Chief was known to go skinny-dipping in the Potomac River in the dead of winter and to take hell-for-leather horseback rides through D.C.'s Rock Creek Park, squeezing off shots from his pistol at trees, twigs, and visiting ambassadors if they didn't get out of his way fast enough.

Much to the chagrin of his family, close friends, and traveling companions, he expected no less enthusiasm from the people around him for all things athletic. Eventually, this attitude filtered into his views on the military, when the scion of Oyster Bay suggested that each American under arms should be able to cover fifty miles in the course of twenty hours. Militarily, this made a lot of sense, especially in the days before helicopters. No less than Napoleon Bonaparte and the brilliant Confederate general Robert E. Lee were known for marching their men over dazzling distances to launch immediate attacks, which sent foes scrambling into retreat.

But it took many decades and changes in the Oval Office before Roosevelt's idea came to practical life. In the spring of 1963, President John Kennedy resurrected Teddy's bold notion as part of his great push to promote physical fitness. That year a series of fifty-mile races was launched across the country to make people get out, get busy, and get fit. They were military races, but as regular runners heard about them, they wanted in. Then autumn came, the young president went to Dallas, and everything changed.

As the nation went into mourning, enthusiasm faded for the races inspired by the assassinated president. The only race to survive was the one close to D.C. It was rechristened as the JFK 50 Mile, and ever since it has drawn fields of highly fit troops and civilians alike to test their mettle against the great course.

The idea of joining such storied company appealed to me, although the mileage was monumental. Stacking up a few marathons and halves was one thing; taking on a monster like this was another matter entirely. I didn't know how to get ready. In terms of training, nutrition, sleep, and equipment, the JFK 50 was a great mystery.

Something else I did not know: The sport does not tolerate hesitation. I assumed few people would even consider competing in something so difficult. "There can't be that many," I said to Linda in the car as I was once again discussing the possibility of entering. "I mean, you wouldn't expect to find a line of people pushing each other out of the way to get whacked on the head with a bat, would you? I imagine they just barely fill the race each year."

I was badly mistaken. It turns out that ultrarunners are re-markably enthusiastic.

When I finally got around to reading the details about en-tering the JFK 50 on its website, I was stunned. While it did not have qualifying times like the Boston Marathon, runners with the best previous times for marathons or ultras were al-lowed to enter first. If they didn't fill all the slots, then the next wave of slightly slower runners were allowed to sign up. And only then would the rest of us be allowed to give it a go. Months ahead of the race, I was already too late. The JFK 50 was full for that year, and I was sent back to musing about running a superlong race elsewhere.

That did not exactly bother me. I continued telling myself that the idea of running an ultra was nothing more than a lark. I enjoyed reading about people splashing through leech-filled swamps and thundering down mountainsides so hard that their femurs cracked. I was fascinated by stories of blisters that bled through shoes, men and women who grew delirious with effort and tumbled into abandoned mines, and athletes im-mersing themselves in tubs of ice to lower their off-the-chart core temperatures. But it was runner porn: something to titil-late my imagination and to minimize on the computer screen if anyone strolled by. Fifty Shades of Blisters.

Nonetheless, even after the JFK disappointment, I drifted to websites that explained how regular runners (like me) could transform themselves into super runners (not at all like me) in a matter of months; how bodies could be recast as high-performance engines, fueled by sports drinks and protein and capable of grinding down even the greatest distances. I read stories of remote tribes that ran for days on nothing but a handful of corn and wearing sandals woven from plants. I read about trail-devouring beasts who ran on their own rocket-fuel mixes of cupcakes, beer, and raw oats. Or something like that. I read dozens of theories about how to cover these monumental distances—some the heart of simplicity, some as complicated as the tax code. The bottom line in every article and book was the same unambiguous message I'd heard in the office from Lisa: You can do this.

Still, I had serious doubts. One Sunday, during my weekly phone call with Robert, I bought up the subject again.

"I keep thinking about these ultras," I told him. "I just can't imagine anyone running that far."

"Sure you can," he said. "Don't you remember how a 10K once seemed huge? How the marathon seemed impossible? This is the same thing. You just have to go after it, commit, and train like hell."

"I don't know. I've looked at some training plans, and I don't think I'm ready."

"Let me ask a question: At your age, do you think you're going to be more ready next year?"

Ronnie echoed the idea. "Look, Dad, you can't let all that training just fade away now. Remember what you told me after I had that bad run back in January?"

"I think I told you that baby powder would help with the chafing."

"No. The other thing. You said, 'Don't worry about reaching the end of your run. Just focus on the next step.' That's what you need to do now."

It seemed impossible. Ultrarunners aren't simply "out there" compared with most other humans. In a long run, the most talented ones would destroy even the best professional athletes from other sports.

Consider professional football players. It's estimated that even running backs and receivers cover a paltry 1.25 miles from the opening kickoff to the final whistle. Though a routine game might last three hours, the majority of that time is lost in huddles, penalties, time-outs, video reviews, and TV breaks to show cheerleaders and sell beer. Most plays last only six or seven seconds. A player would have to be on the field for every down in fifty straight games, in a "hurry up" offense both ways, with no halftime, no two-minute warning, no pauses of any kind, to be on the move as much as even a middling ultrarunner.

Baseball players? Forget it. Most of their time on the field consists of standing, scratching, and waiting for a brief, wildly explosive moment in which they might cover a dozen yards. Okay, the outfielders could go twice as far, but that's still not much.

An analysis by Gizmodo.com had even the busiest basketball players covering a scant two to three miles. Tennis players, in really long matches, were given credit for up to five miles. And professional soccer players, while commonly covering seven miles per game, still ran less than a quarter of the distance involved in the smallest ultra. True, most of these other sports involve explosive running that is physically demanding in its own way, but ultrarunners nonetheless have staked a corner at the intersection of endurance and pain where few outsiders dare venture.

All that has left insurance brokers and doctors scratching

their heads over what to make of the super-long-distance crowd. One of the most extensive studies to date was conducted by the University of California, Davis, and Stanford University. In extensive interviews with 1,200 ultramarathoners, researchers concluded that these runners are pretty darn healthy—and they sneeze a lot.

The healthy part: All that running appears to reduce the likelihood of heart disease, diabetes, high blood pressure, and cancer. The sneezy part: Ultrarunners spend a lot more time in the woods than most people, brushing against trees, bushes, flowers, and weeds while their lungs are hoovering up all the air, pollen, dust, and small bugs they can suck in. So, surprise, they're more likely to suffer from exercise-induced asthma and allergies.

A few other details have emerged. Ultra folks seldom miss work for illness, and they don't see doctors often. Maybe that's because they're not sick, or maybe it's because they get so used to dealing with pain that they just don't notice it anymore. Ultrarunners suffer small injuries on a regular basis: twisted ankles, stubbed toes, scraped knees, and the like. But here is a fun fact: Younger runners are more likely to be hurt. Maybe it's because they attack the courses with too much enthusiasm or lack the experience to navigate the varied terrain, or maybe they run too long on minor problems, turning them into major ones. Whatever the cause, it is well established that older runners dominate in ultras in ways that they could never hope to in shorter races. Indeed, the advantage held by so-called master runners steadily grows with race length, so much so that many strong twentysomethings are stunned late in long races to see people who could be their grandparents leaving them in the dust.

The more I read about all this, the more it enticed me in a perverse way. That night, sitting in the family room watching TV with Linda, I found another race online. The Stone Mill 50 started and ended only a half hour from my house. I knew some of the woods through which it ran. It was scheduled for the weekend before Thanksgiving, the same day as the JFK 50 and just days shy of the one-year anniversary of Ronnie's dragging me into this running odyssey. It seemed like kismet. How could I pass this up?

I sat on the sofa filling in all the blanks on the entry form, my stomach knotted with doubt. I punched in my credit card info. I reached the final line and stared at the screen, wondering whether this was the right thing to do or the thing that would ruin all that I had done.

"Still not sure?" Linda asked.

I looked at her and shook my head. She'd had plenty of fears all along my journey, and she'd never hesitated to caution me about overreaching. But somehow she must have seen something in that moment that I did not. She leaned over, kissed me on the cheek, and pressed Send. "Now you are."

THIRTEEN

Where the hell are you going?" Linda asked. We had pulled to the side of the road beside an unbroken line of woods ten miles from home. To judge from the Stone Mill website, the race was fifty miles of hills, creeks, deer trails, and bitter cold, and I knew my training had to begin right here, right now, or I'd never be ready by autumn.

"In there," I said, nodding toward the trees.

"How?" She had good-naturedly encouraged my dementia, but this was not in the bargain. She stared at the forest as if it were the thicket of thorns around Sleeping Beauty's castle.

"There is a trail," I said, "at least the map online says so. It's just around that big tree, and I'm pretty sure it will eventually take me to the towpath."

"How long is this trail of yours?"

"About two miles. Or eight. I'm not sure."

"Or fifteen or twenty? Or maybe you'll wind up in Virginia and have no idea how you got there?"

"Don't be silly," I said. "I'd have to swim the Potomac. I'd notice that right away."

I feigned nonchalance, but I knew I was jumping into an

entirely different experience. Ultra races, aside from being much longer than most runs, are most often not on broad, flat, safe courses that have been marked off for your comfort and pleasure. Ultras are commonly trail races. They go through woods, over mountains, down gullies, across creeks, and under bridges. The path might be rock, dirt, mud, sand, gravel, snow, ice, or waist-deep water. You might clamber up a sheer stone face or slide down a thistle-strewn cliff. The courses are often marked with little more than chalk blazes on rocks or ribbons hanging from trees, and getting lost is, if not a sure bet, at least a real possibility. In other words, everything that is potentially dangerous about running a marathon increases exponentially in the ultra world.

A cursory look at the online warnings for these hellish races reveals an extravagant grab bag of life-threatening features. Renal failure from the extended distance can leave you urinating blood at best, looking for a kidney donor at worst. Muscle necrosis can reduce your well-trained legs to quivering masses of dying cells, which will take months to recover if they do at all. Falling trees can splinter your bones. Mudslides can dislocate your hips. Roots can snap your ankles. Rock slides can sweep you into eternity, or leave you with the nickname "Hopalong" for the rest of your days. Every element of these races seems prefaced with the word *extreme*—extreme cold, extreme heat, extreme exhaustion, extreme delusions, extreme convulsions, extreme death. It's all out there hiding with rattlesnakes, mountain lions, coyotes, skunks, bears, porcupines, badgers, water moccasins, Gila monsters, hornets, scorpions, and just about anything else you can imagine waiting in the wilderness for an idiot to stumble past.

That said, there are several reasons for ultras to be out in the woods where sane folks fear to tread. First, it cuts down on road closures, which tend to piss off the neighbors—and considering that these races routinely take twelve hours or more, that's no small matter. Second, the runners like the courses this way. Running down a nice, clean stretch of asphalt brings higher speeds, less risk of injury, and easier access to aid stations. It's also boring. When you're running from sunup to sundown, it's nice to see something other than the next traffic light. And third, if you're going to do something this stupid, you don't want too many witnesses.

At least that's what I thought on that initial morning.

Stepping into the woods is one thing. Going there to run is like entering an alternate universe. Instantly, the dappled light turned into an enemy, masking all manner of dips, ridges, and debris. Briars slashed my legs. I bobbed my head to avoid branches. My knees torqued into positions reserved for masochistic yoga instructors. My ankles twisted, and my heart hammered. Everything felt foreign as I attempted running up and down trails designed for hiking with boots, maps, compasses, and armies of Eagle Scouts.

All my foot placements were wrong. My toes slammed into rocks and roots. I tripped. I fell. Over and over. My glasses were slapped off by saplings. I flailed at invisible spiderwebs. I got lost, doubled back, and got lost again. When I finally burst from the woods to the safety of the towpath forty-five minutes later, I had traveled what I would later calculate to be only 3.5 hapless miles. It felt like twenty, and I looked like a member of the Donner Party. I had twigs hanging from my hair. My knees and hands were covered with scratches and caked with grime. I was cursing the trees, the dirt, and the birds. I passed a family out for a stroll and grunted, "How's it going?"

"Great!" the parents said as they pushed their two children behind them. I could tell what they meant. *"Oh, we're fine, but we're pretty sure you're as nutty as Donald Trump at a toupee parlor. Now, if you'll excuse us, we're going to go apply for a concealed-carry permit."*

I jogged the remaining miles in a dark mood as I considered the twin challenges that were woefully apparent. I needed to step my mileage up. Way up. From around 40 miles a week to 60, 70, 80, or more before the race came. And I had to master the tricks of trail running, for which I apparently had no aptitude.

That first challenge came covered with warning flags. Nothing raises the probability of injury faster than increasing your mileage too quickly. Muscles, ligaments, cartilage, and bones are remarkably resilient. They can be strained nearly to the breaking point, stretched to their limits, and they can come back stronger. The basis of all exercise is this push-pull of effort and recovery. But the greater the effort, the more recovery that's required. So if you've been tooling along at six miles a day and you shift gears to sixteen, even if you have the stamina to pull it off, your body will revolt. Aches will appear in places you've never dreamed. Twinges will shoot through you as if Nikola Tesla were your dentist. Cramps will strike muscles in the middle of the night, causing overly ambitious runners to leap from their beds shrieking, "Holy Mother of God, kill me now!" Which, I might add, more than a few runners' spouses have been tempted to follow up on.

I once read an article about the Kenyan Olympic team's training regimen. It went into great detail about their otherworldly schedule. Wake at dawn to cover ten miles, a short break, then six more miles up and down the side of a mountain, another break, and then a late-day run of ten more miles. Something like that. It was exhausting to read, and contemplating doing it made my muscles sympathetically throb. The writer argued that this fierce training is what makes the Kenyans such magnificent runners, but he also included a warning. The same training that creates champions can destroy them as well. The mileage and intensity ruined some promising athletes by inducing injuries from which they would never recover.

Although I was no Kenyan, I understood. The single biggest problem that had plagued all my past attempts to get serious about running was precisely this. I would begin my training well. Soon I would start feeling good. I would jack up my mileage, and worse, when trouble started to appear, I would try to push through it. Eventually, I would end up limping home one afternoon, ready to throw my shoes into the trash and take up Scrabble. My injuries had never been permanent, but they had lasted long enough to repeatedly crush my hopes of a comeback. Knees. Toes. Shins. Hips. I could not let that happen this time. Studying the calendar after dinner, I scowled.

"Troubles, Dad?"

Ali had just sailed in on the good ship *Mockery*.

"Looks that way. What day is this?"

"Saturday. Middle of August," she said.

"That's not good."

"It is for me. School doesn't start again for two weeks. What's up?"

"I have to run this race in November, and I'm not sure I can get trained in time."

"How about this? I'll overlook you using the words 'have to,' and you can overlook me staying out half the night with my friends."

"If I try to stick to this schedule," I said, "I'll have to cut all sorts of corners to even come close to the proper mileage. I'll have to expand all my routes dramatically, decrease my work-to-rest ratio, and run faster the whole time. I don't think I can handle it."

Ali's expression shifted as she realized that I was genuinely concerned. She smiled kindly. Despite her love of all things snarky, she knew this mattered to me. She came over and draped an arm across my shoulders. "If you don't mind me saying so: first-world problem. And besides, you've been running a ton."

"The race is fifty miles long."

"Wow!" Her eyes widened. "You're doing this on purpose? You know I love you, Dad, and if there was any way I could help, I would. But short of finding a psychiatrist online, I can only wish you luck. Anyway, you can do it. You know you can. And on that note, I'm going for pizza with my friends. Happy trails!"

Doubt is a constant companion of long-distance runners. We're always wondering if we are training too hard or too soft. If we are running too many hills or not enough. We worry about finishing too slowly, and we fret about whether we will finish at all. From the first day that I laced on my shoes, through all the training and through the Atlanta marathon it-self, nagging uncertainty had always been there. Now it was worse than ever before. I needed someone who understood.

Ronnie was home for the summer but pulling long hours at an internship. We were enjoying relatively few long runs together, and yet she was proving an invaluable inspiration and guide through the process. She talked about how, during her grueling aerospace finals, she'd remembered the lessons of perseverance and toughness she'd picked up in the marathon. Staring at equations the size of Escalades, she'd put her head down and calculate like a banshee. She still called seeking moral support late at night when she'd studied so long that she was crumbling with exhaustion, but her calls were no longer tinged with the hysteria we'd once known. And more than once those conversations had devolved into running meta-phors: "This is mile 19," or "You have to pace yourself," or "Here comes the home stretch."

I shot an e-mail to her at the office with the subject line "HELP!" I quickly explained my growing sense of panic and asked, "Do you have any advice for an old running buddy?"

Her reply came so quickly it was as if she had been sitting there waiting for my crisis. "While we were getting ready for our marathon," she wrote, "I was afraid a lot. I was afraid of getting embarrassed, getting hurt, and getting lost. I was afraid I'd give up on training, or drop out of the race. Most of all, I was afraid of letting you down. I knew you would push through because I had asked you to, but sometimes I honestly didn't believe I could. I didn't think I could face all those fears. I didn't think there was a world in which I could run like my dad. I've learned there is, and maybe I am as tough as you've always said I could be. That's a big part of what I got out of that race, and in my worst moments I remembered some great words: If it is inevitable, it is ideal."

She was quoting an aphorism I had said to her since her youngest days. I've never been able to trace its origin, but I've thought of it countless times on the job as I've faced angry policemen, even angrier protesters, armed thugs, or even more heavily armed soldiers. Or worst of all, when I've been staring down the barrel of a deadline. When I've been tempted to complain about the unreasonableness of the universe, I've remembered those words. They are my private clarion call to quit screwing around and get busy solving the problem. They tell me that the ground on which you are standing, no matter where it might be, is the perfect place to take a stand.

I was a single run into my new training plan, and I was mentally giving up. In my mind, I was still not a real athlete. I was still battling to overcome my years, my weight, and the nagging desire to quit. I was still a guy who feared he was way out of his element. In one sentence, Ronnie brought me back.

There was no crawfishing out of Stone Mill now without incurring a DNF, and after the glorious resurrection of my running career, I could not let that happen. Therefore, I could not see the training as a burden. I needed to see it as an opportunity. Whether I liked it or not, I was signed up and the race was coming.

It was inevitable.

That made it ideal.

FOURTEEN

Over the next couple of weeks, I hit the same trails repeatedly. I kept falling. I kept twisting my ankles and knees in all sorts of unpleasant ways. I kept cursing nature as if it were my personal enemy. Which, when you think about it, is true for all of us. Gradually, I improved.

"You know," I told Linda one morning as she dropped me off, "I realized that there isn't just one trail near here. There are dozens of them!"

"Uh-huh," she said, as if this weren't intrinsically fascinating.

"They cross, and loop, and stop, and start, all over the woods. Some of them actually lead to pretty cool places."

"Like?"

"Like to a scenic overlook."

She eyed the tangle of woods. "Nothing looks all that scenic in there."

"It's relative. You know how we always say your cousin Nicky is pretty? You know that's only compared to her corgis, right?"

"I get your point."

"Anyway, some of the other paths just lead off to nothing.

You follow them, and gradually they fade out until you're just lost in the weeds, wondering where the hell you are."

"I guess that makes us even."

"What?"

"Every time you take off into that mess, I wonder the same thing: Where the hell is he? Is he coming back? How much will the funeral cost?"

I dismissed her wisecracks, but I understood. Just a few weeks earlier I had tried branching off into a new area, following a promising trail past a little creek, up a hill, and into oblivion. As smoothly as a magician's trick, the path vanished beneath me. I looked ahead: nothing. Behind: nothing. I had no idea when I'd left the trail or where it had gone. I trotted on, pushing branches aside and peering into the underbrush for any hint about where I belonged, and finally stumbled into a clearing, where I found two lost hikers. They looked worried.

"Where is the trail?" I asked.

"We thought you might know," they responded.

Another day I had blasted out of the woods and into a camping site, rumbling up on a tent full of people who shrieked as if a bear had charged from the mountain laurel. There were a few cryptic old signposts, which were as useful as Egyptian hieroglyphics. Still, I began sorting out all those paths in the woods—sometimes by their condition, sometimes by landmarks, and sometimes with a growing sense of the forest itself. A step at a time, the right way just started looking right.

"I didn't get lost! Not even once!" I crowed to the family one day as I burst, sweating and dusty, through the front door. "I came to that same series of forks where I always go wrong, and

I remembered this big rock next to two trees and knew I had to go left, and then I saw the creek, turned right at the log, climbed over that boulder, saw the rotting hut, reconnected to the towpath, and here I am!"

"Good for you," Linda said.

"Nice," said Ronnie.

Ali smiled. "Way to go, Magellan."

The miles added up. Training runs that are on the long side for marathons are mere warm-ups when you're preparing for an ultra, and that makes for some hefty entries in the running log. The challenge I'd recognized back in winter with the marathon was growing exponentially greater with the ultra; to wit, how to fit all that training time into my life?

"How many miles today?" became the endless query, whether from Linda, who wanted to discuss household affairs, or from Ali, who might want homework help, or from Ronnie, who sometimes would venture to join me on shorter sections when her internship gave her time. The daily answer went steadily up: 20 miles, 23, 25, and more. I would launch in the early morning, backtiming everything to allow for feeding the dog, getting ready for work, doing my job, and coming home to eat, sleep, and do it all again the next day. The math was formidable. Consider that on particularly good days I might rip along at 6 to 7 miles an hour, or as I like to think of it, somewhat less than half the speed of the marathon world-record holder. At that rate, a 20-mile run takes well over three hours. It was like making time to watch *Gone with the Wind* each morning before breakfast.

The long days of summer gave me more time in which I could pound down miles without feeling as if I'd lost the whole day to running. My technique was improving, and that helped too. I learned to use smooth, short strides that barely took my feet off the ground when I headed uphill. It was a muscle-saving maneuver akin to dropping a bicycle into low gear, and it proved invaluable as I ground my way up rocky slopes and dirt inclines. On the descents, I learned to relax, unleash my legs, and "bomb" down to the valley floor, letting gravity do most of the work. Through it all, I scrutinized the terrain like never before for logs that might roll beneath me, branches that might snap and cut into my calves, rocks that might skitter if I used them to cross a creek, and clumps of cattails that might erupt with the heart-stopping rush of a great blue heron.

"I feel like the last of the Mohicans," I told Linda.

"You mean Daniel Day-Lewis? I'm not seeing that."

"No, the other guys. The Mohicans who were with him."

"Like the one who pushes the girl over the cliff? He was horrible."

"She jumped. And no, that was Magua. He was a Huron. Remember the two guys who were with Daniel Day-Lewis all the time? Those guys."

"So, you're the old chief?"

"No. I'm the young, handsome one."

"Ah, that's why I'm confused."

"Anyway, I'm learning to read the signs of the forest."

"That will be helpful when the French invade. Can you build a canoe?"

"Did I ever tell you that somewhere way back in my family line there is a Native American?"

"You neglected to mention that."

"Or maybe someone in our family married one. Or met one.

Or saw one in a movie. I'm not sure. Anyway, I'm learning to recognize all sorts of birdcalls and different types of trees, and I've even noticed some mushrooms I've never seen before."

"Are you eating them? Because you sound like you're hallucinating."

"You're a funny gal," I said.

"Did I tell you that I'm descended from an ancient tribe?" she replied. "We were called the Unimpressed. We were known for hunting, trapping, and ridicule."

Something primordial was at work in me. I found myself thinking about all the great writers who had explored the notion of getting back to nature, chief among them Henry David Thoreau. I had never really been a fan. He prattles on for pages about the wonders of a simple house without all that bothersome furniture that his neighbors have cluttered their places up with in the 1850s, but then on the next page he's bragging, "Look, I made a La-Z-Boy recliner with nothing but my ax!"

He also praises the virtues of solitude so much that you'd think he was a hermit. Then he writes a whole passage about going to town, catching up on gossip, stopping by the bank, and picking up his dry cleaning. Earlier in the year, Ali had been assigned *Walden* for an English class, and I decided to page through it with her just to see if my opinion of Thoreau might be improved. It wasn't.

"For a guy who says he wants to be alone, he seems to have an awful lot of company," Ali said.

"Kind of like *Gilligan's Island*. They're supposedly all alone, but people are always dropping by," I said.

"I don't know what you're talking about."

"It was a TV show."

"Thoreau didn't have a TV."

"Never mind."

"And how can anyone write so much about a pond? Seriously."

Like I said, I wasn't a fan. But pounding through the trees every day for such long periods, I was beginning to wonder whether Thoreau was onto something after all. One of the great pleasures of ultrarunning is that it allows time for reflection, including stops to enjoy the scenery and wildlife. Maybe for all his strange ways, this is what he meant by "I never found a companion that was so companionable as solitude."

Raccoons and foxes skipped along the trails, leaving paw prints in the sand and mud. Turtles wallowed in the canal, piled on logs to dry, and turned dusty white in the sun. Blue and green lizards shot across my path. Snakes stretched across rocks. A bright orange salamander wiggled down under a rotting stump. Running along a bog with Ronnie in tow, we saw a couple of pale, lavender-white blobs suspended under the surface. Dropping to our knees in the squishy grass, we tried to make out what they were. They looked like pieces of waterlogged Styrofoam.

"Look. They're everywhere," Ronnie said.

There were dozens. Each as big as double fists. I pushed a hand into the cool depths and gently pulled one up to inspect it.

"It's an egg sack," Ronnie told me excitedly. "Frogs! Those will be tadpoles soon!"

Runners encounter all sorts of critters. One friend literally ran into a deer while out in the deep twilight, thumping into the animal's flank at a dead run and scaring the hell out of both of them. And on any given day, I'd find small herds dashing alongside me through the trees.

Once, a magnificent pileated woodpecker swept up to the green canopy above me, and I stopped for a full five minutes to watch it hammer at a hole in a dead tree, making way for a nest. On other days, flurries of bluebirds appeared like something from a Disney film. Jays and goldfinches shot among the leaves. Green herons crouched like old men waiting for minnows. Kingfishers swooped ahead, always retreating as soon as I came close enough for a good look.

One warm evening, as Ronnie and I were racing out of some remote woods before dark, I saw a tall figure moving. We were running quickly and quietly, and it didn't see us until we pulled up behind it on the narrow path. Turned out, "it" was a nature lover—a very tall, very happy, very naked man.

"I'm sorry," he said, turning to face us squarely in the dusky light, "it's just so nice out tonight I couldn't help myself. Isn't nature magnificent?"

I mumbled something before we breezed past and ran the final mile in silence, glancing over our shoulders. Inside the car, I started the engine, looked into the now dark woods, and said, "'Isn't nature magnificent?' Is that what he said?"

"Yeah," Ronnie replied. "But I saw his nature, and it wasn't that great."

We laughed all the way home.

I encountered an endless and bewildering variety of vegetation, most of which I knew nothing about. Of course, I collided with the usual suspects: thornbushes that tore at my legs, whip-thin saplings that striped my arms, and on one notable occasion a sycamore that dropped a large branch a few feet from where I was passing. There were also all sorts of magical plants doing things I never knew of, or perhaps never noticed before. I ran into clusters of droopy-headed weeds, which exploded at my touch, spraying tiny seeds in all directions. Huge, spreading fungi appeared overnight and disappeared in a day sporting outrageous splashes of pink, yellow, red, and creamy white. Plain bushes that I'd passed dozens of times would one day be covered with a lacework of minuscule blossoms. More wildflowers than I could count appeared alongside my feet: tiny white ones, and waxy yellow ones, and sparking purple ones, and at the right time, the bluebells nodded dreamily over every inch alongside the path.

More than all of that, however, I came to know the weather.

Most of our modern lives, as Thoreau lamented well before air-conditioning, are spent cosseted from the elements. Our houses, offices, stadiums, restaurants, and malls are fortresses against inclemency of all types. We have dual climate controls in our cars so we don't have to endure a degree of disagreement with our traveling companions. We buy beds with thermostatically controlled heaters, and we install ceiling fans to move the conditioned air through the room at comfortable intervals. Mind you, all this does not keep my wife and daughters from remarking even in the heat of August, "It's cold in here!"

Stores that ostensibly cater to outdoor enthusiasts sell all manner of gear designed to keep the outdoors from getting too close. For summer, there are high-tech rain suits with sealable waists and cuffs, waterproof boots, heat-monitoring tops, and heat-releasing bottoms. For winter, there are temperature-controlled gloves, convertible hats to maintain the ideal ratio of heating to cooling, and jackets with so many layers of tech-wear that if Shackleton had had such gear, he probably would have stayed at the South Pole.

"Sir Ernest! We are the rescue party sent to bring you home!"

"Oh, no, thanks. Please tell the queen we're doing quite well. Look, my jacket is made of Gore-Tex!"

Unlike cyclists, who seem to have no end of interest in buying products related to their sport, ultrarunners have no truck with such things. Beyond shoes, shorts, and a top layer or two, it is simply impractical for trail runners to get tied up in a lot of specialized gear. Once the basics are in place, anything else is unnecessary weight. So if it is cold, we run faster to raise our core temperature. If it is hot, we slow down. If it rains, we get wet. If it snows, we get wet and we sneeze. Along the way, we develop a sense of what's coming next. Like old farmers on the Great Plains, ultrarunners have an internal barometer, sussing out from the clouds, the time, and the smell of the air what is likely to happen in the next few hours. Also helpful: a smart phone with a weather app.

Not that any forecast matters much. Seldom do serious ultrarunners alter their plans because of the weather. Rather, we take the legendary advice of the amorous old Scottish husband to his wife: "Brace yourself!"

I ran with thunderstorms raking the hillsides and exploding above the trees. (Yes, I realize this was stupid.) I ran with wind shrieking through the branches and buffeting me so hard that I thought I might fall over. (Yes, this was stupid too.) I ran in unseasonable cold, and I ran in such blinding heat that I couldn't drink enough, no matter how I tried, and descended into dehydration and heat exhaustion. This, I was learning, is the way of the ultra.

Complicating everything was the matter of work. Against the expanding schedule, I could see my life rapidly devolving into a three-legged stool: running, working, and sleeping. Linda did not complain. We would enjoy rambling conversations about the kids, movies, the house, and more as she drove me to remote drop-off points. Then we would ease to a stop by some barely visible path through the trees, and she'd smile sweetly and say, "This was fun. Now get out."

But everyone knew that time with Dad was in short supply, and like news families around the world, we also knew the priority ranking. Work could not be shortchanged. People at CNN were counting on me. And as much as they were amused by my extracurriculars, when news breaks, someone has to fix it. I was reminded of an old joke that is popular in newsrooms.

A reporter, a cameraman, and a producer are shipwrecked on an island. One of them finds a magic lamp, and out pops a genie, who says, "I'll give each of you a wish."

The reporter says, "I'd like a manor in the French countryside, a garage full of sports cars, and a beautiful girlfriend." Poof. He is gone.

The cameraman says, "I'd like a home in the mountains, with a perpetually filled beer fridge, and great skiing all year-round." Poof. He disappears.

"And what can I do for you?" the genie asks the producer.

"Get those guys back here," the producer says. "We have work to do!"

The potential clashes between work and running revolve around a four-letter word: time. Running takes time. Work does too. If they both want the same time, trouble follows. When I joined ABC's *World News Tonight* in 1990, it was rid-ing high in the ratings, and I was the youngest correspondent on Peter Jennings's team. My age and limited experience raised eyebrows, with Peter even saying, "Maybe we should have a little gray put into your hair." Accordingly, I fretted over rookie mistakes, the first of which came from running.

Although I was based in Denver, I had been called out to Los Angeles one weekend to fill in for a vacationing correspondent. I went to the ABC bureau on the east end of Hollywood ready for anything to happen, but nothing did. By Saturday afternoon, Derek, the guy on the assignment desk, was urging me to head out. "You have a pager. We don't even have a show until Sunday night. Go see the sights."

The next morning after breakfast, I put on exercise clothes and drove to Santa Monica for a rare run by the Pacific Ocean. The paved path wound invitingly alongside beachside shops and through a California mix of bikini-clad skaters, jugglers, street musicians, sun worshippers, and volleyball players. I ran around a parade of a hundred or more Hare Krishnas banging tambourines as their painted elephant lumbered along. It was lovely. After three miles I turned around, and right then, when I was the farthest from the bureau that I'd been at any other moment in the weekend, my pager went off. I trotted to a pay phone.

"Hi, Tom. It's Derek. ABC Sports unexpectedly wrapped up coverage of a golf tournament. Rain or something. New York did a five-minute news segment to fill the gap, but when the West Coast feed hits, we'll need to update it here. So head this way."

"How fast?"

"You've got time. We don't have to be ready for a few hours."

I continued running comfortably, and I was still twenty minutes away from my rental car when the pager went off again.

"Hi, Tom. It's Derek. Turns out that we have to do that update in an hour."

I dropped into a sprint, dodging around strollers, surfers, and the saffron-robed Krishnas, shouting, "Sorry! Look out! Sorry, sorry!" By the time I reached the car, I was sweating like I was in the throes of a thyroid storm. I was practically up on two wheels as I ripped around corners, cut off other drivers, and screeched up to the hotel to grab a suit, shirt, and tie. Back in the car, I changed as I drove, trying to dry my hair with an air-conditioning vent. At one point I executed an illegal U-turn that would have made a movie stuntman proud. It was all for nothing. I reached the newsroom two minutes after the window for our newsbreak was over. Derek had rustled up a reporter from the local ABC station to fill in for me. I collapsed into a chair, lamenting the loss of my still-new job, which I felt was inevitable.

"Where were you?" the bureau chief, Kathy, asked when she called a bit later.

"I was running. In Santa Monica."

"You probably shouldn't be that far away again."

I was so grateful that she hadn't fired me that I stayed perched in the newsroom for the next seven hours, filthy, hungry, and with my hair looking as if it had been styled in a blender. I had learned my lesson about the demands of national news.

Occasional mistakes still came nonetheless. After I left ABC to help start the National Geographic Channel, I was once again out in California, this time for an interview with

Gerald Ford to discuss his legacy. The former president was meeting us at a resort near his home in Rancho Mirage, and my crew and producer spent the afternoon setting up the cameras, microphones, and lights. I reread a thick binder of research and decided to relax with a short run. The resort was in the middle of the Coachella Valley, and the landscape was wide open. Small cacti clustered around low scrub, creosote plants, and sandy patches. I set off on an easy trail, planning on three miles at most. The sun was hidden behind thin clouds, but nonetheless, after twenty minutes I was hot. I spotted a dirt road leading back to the hotel, and I thought I would hop down onto it. What I didn't know was the degree to which the gray light had flattened the landscape. The moment I jumped, I realized that the dirt road was not ten inches down but rather four feet beneath me. I ran in space, spun my arms, and crashed. Blood oozed from my right knee, congealing in the dirt on my leg. I limped back to the resort, showered, and wrapped my wound with lengths of toilet paper while watching the clock.

By the time Ford, arrived my leg was stiff, and I was wincing at each step. He shook my hand and snarled, "I suppose you're going to bring up that old question about why I pardoned Nixon again."

"We're going to cover a lot of topics, Mr. President," I said.

The interview lasted nearly an hour, and despite his advancing age, Ford displayed a keen mind and memory. If his eyes had been equally sharp, he might have seen the blood seeping through my makeshift bandage and trousers.

That was not the only athletic mishap. One memorable election night at CNN in New York, my producer Katie and I had taken up residence in the offices of the *Anderson Cooper 360°* show. Phones were ringing. Other producers and corre-spondents were swirling. Erica Hill, these days with *Today*, was in her office just yards away. In the studio, our anchors and analysts were waiting for returns to come in. The rest of us were killing time. Turning to an excellent producer named Mary Anne Fox, who I knew was always up for an adventure, I proposed a wager.

"I'll bet you a quarter that I can stand flat-footed and jump up onto that desk."

The desk was of normal height, I was wearing a suit with loafers, and I'd had more than my share from the pizza boxes piled on the desks. Mary Anne smiled mischievously and said, "You're on."

I'd made this wager many times, and I'd never failed to collect. The secret was to get a smooth launch, with a steady sweep of the arms for extra height, and then snap the feet forward onto the surface. A small, curious crowd gathered. The backs of my legs felt tight from a run the previous day, but I thought nothing of it. I took off my jacket, crouched, and jumped. For a tenth of a second the toes of my shoes caught the top of the desk, and a spontaneous cheer began. Then they popped loose, I rocketed downward, and my shins slammed into the metal edge. The crash brought Erica run-ning, wide-eyed. "What on earth happened?" she said, while everyone laughed.

"I'm fine," I said, "but that's going to hurt tomorrow."

The shock was so intense that the initial sensation was numbness. I wanted to see how badly I'd bruised myself, so I lifted my pant legs, and the laughter turned to shrieks. Blood was pouring down from deep gashes, pooling on my shoes, and overflowing onto the carpet. A friend on the staff, Mona Mouallem, called her father, who was a doctor and lived close by. He looked over my wounds, wrapped them in gauze, and said, "You're going to need something more." I did my live shot, and once again, discerning eyes could have seen the blood soaking through my suit. Then Katie and I hiked over to Roosevelt Hospital, where a few stitches were laced into each shin.

Over time, my collected clashes between running and work made me keep a close eye on upcoming news events and plan my runs around them. If the White House was announcing a big jobs initiative at 10:00 a.m., I was out on the running path well before dawn. If Congress was holding an all-day hearing on trade with the Chinese, I'd trudge the trails deep into the night. Yet conflicts arose despite my efforts. My days at the studio tend to run late into the evening, so I typically arrive at the office between 9:00 and 10:30 in the morning. I was planning on hitting the back edge of that envelope one day as I was working through a dozen miles on rough trails down by the Potomac. The morning was warm and the sun was shining. The river was sparkling and my legs felt bouncy as I sprang up and down the hills, thoughts of work a million miles away. Then my phone rang.

"Hey," said Eric Sherling, one of our bureau execs most closely tied to my work in our special Virtual Studio, used for explaining complex ideas and situations. "Have you heard about Iran?"

"No."

"Where are you?"

"In the woods. Running."

"They've announced some more missile stuff. Keep running. Let me find out a little more."

He hung up. The Iranians had been making headlines for months with both their ballistic missile and nuclear programs. I had emerged as CNN's unofficial "explainer in chief," telling our viewers about the development of the nuclear plants, as well as the number of missiles and their design, range, and warhead capabilities. We had built elaborate computer-generated scenes to illustrate all this, and I mentally reviewed our inventory of facts and images as I cranked off another mile before Eric rang again.

"How soon can you be here?"

I looked around, sweat dripping, my brain flashing back to that day in L.A. Nothing but trees, dirt, and water all around. I had four miles to go, which would translate into a half hour even if I went all out. Then I'd have to shower, dress, and navigate ten miles of D.C. traffic to our office near the Capitol.

"I think I'm at least an hour out," I told him. "Let me work on it."

I hung up and dialed Linda.

"What's up?" she said, surprised to hear from me in the midst of a run.

I replied with a question she hadn't heard in all the months of training. "Can you come get me?"

We calculated a bailout point that she could reach by car and I could make on foot. I started moving fast, bushwhacking out of the woods. The next hour was a blur, highlighted by some nasty scratches, the world's fastest shower, and a mercifully smooth commute that had me in the studio on time. I made up for the missing miles later that evening.

My colleagues seemed to find it all simultaneously puzzling and amusing. Wolf would pass me with the question "How far did you go this morning?" The answer grew as the weeks went by: 10 miles, 14 miles, 18 miles. His response never varied. "You're a wild man, Tom Foreman." Coworkers who were runners asked about my routes, injuries, shoes, and diet. Those who were not runners asked me one question above all others, and more often with their eyes than their voices: Why?

It was a question I was asking myself.

FIFTEEN

I have always loved the free, weightless feeling of running in just a shirt and shorts, but a distance runner can easily burn off a pint of fluid in an hour, and on warm days much more. Ultra distances demand a dizzying management of liquids. As much as I hated to do it, the growing mileage forced me to visit a local sporting goods store to purchase a special belt to hold water bottles.

"I'm still not sure why you need this," Ronnie said, fingering the bottles at home and slipping them in and out of their holsters. "You're going to look like a gunfighter."

"I know, but I have to do it. I've been counting on these water fountains along my routes, but I'm running so far these days I can't find enough of them."

"What are you going to fill the bottles with?"

"That's a fair question."

Debates rage on what is best for runners to drink. Lukewarm water, cold water, sports drinks, beer, lemonade, and chocolate milk have all been contenders. In ultrarunning, where sugar consumption is big, there are proponents of Mountain Dew and Coca-Cola. Pick up any running magazine and you're likely to find a beverage debate brewing with strong pros and cons for every proposal.

The proper quantity and quality of fluids is serious business. Miscalculate your intake in a two-hour run and the result could be minimal. Multiply that same mistake by a dozen hours and it can turn cataclysmic. Once the body slips beyond the liquid edge of proper hydration, getting back to normal can be difficult even if you are sitting down. Diminished fluids interfere with the blood's ability to convey oxygen throughout the body, and every effort grows harder. Robbed of life-nourishing liquid, your muscles, internal organs, and even brain start underperforming, and in the worst cases they shut down. The body acts like an old Chevy with a bad radiator.

Then again, even if you carry liquids, you can't just power them down. Many running coaches and sports doctors caution against hyponatremia, or low sodium, caused by the excessive intake of water during exercise, which can also be a performance killer—and a killer in general, as hyponatremia has thrown runners into fatal declines.

So with the purchase of my fluids belt began a series of experiments. I ran with nothing but water. I ran with nothing but sports drinks. I drank mixtures of the two. I ate sports beans with water. I ate beans with sports drinks. I drank every three miles. I waited and drank only after eight or nine miles. I drank every half hour. I drank every fifteen minutes. On it went, an ever-changing series of small tests to see what might work best for me.

"How are things in the lab?" Ali asked as she watched me pour colored liquids into bottles while I squinted at the lines on measuring cups and made notes.

"Okay. Could be better, I guess. Say, you're taking chemistry class, right?" I asked.

"Not that kind of chemistry. You're on your own with this, pal."

Gradually I found the groove that worked for my long runs. I would fill each of my four small plastic bottles with sports drink, and from the moment I left the house, I would drink half of one each half hour. That was enough to get me through four hours of running, by which time I would be tired of sports drink anyway, so I would refill my bottles at a fountain and drink water with sports beans for the remainder of the run. As long as I had to trot into the woods to relieve myself now and then, I knew I was properly hydrated and my muscles stayed, if not bouncy, at least reasonably lively.

Some people say that running makes them feel like teenagers again, and I guess that's true if when you were fifteen, you ate aspirin by the fistful and called anyone who passed you on the trail a "young smartass." While running was generally making me feel better by this point, I was under no illusion that it was a time machine. Injuries last longer as you grow older. Recovery takes more time. And speed, no matter how much you work at it, is a girl waving good-bye from a westbound train. As the years mount, the maximum rate at which our hearts can beat drops, and we slow down. In one specific area, however, I found my ultrarunning pushing back the calendar dramatically: food. After just a few weeks of intense training, I could eat the way I did in high school: burgers, pizzas, cookies, cakes, candy. It made no difference.

"Are you really sure you want all those wings?" Linda asked at a bar and grill.

"I guess I can spare a few . . ."

"No, I don't want one. I'm just wondering if you ought to be powering them down that way."

"I can't help it. I'm crazy hungry."

"Maybe you have a tapeworm."

"Funny. Can you slide that ranch dressing this way?"

Normally a guy my age should be stalking salads, but no matter how much I shoved into my ravenous piehole, I kept dropping weight, and I was always starving. My training sessions were burning 4,000 to 6,000 calories at a pop, and sometimes I'd come in from a long, hot run eight pounds lighter than when I started. Most of that was lost fluids, but not all of it. I was genuinely losing tonnage.

Usually that is far from the case for fifty-year-olds. Weight problems at this age are like in-laws: They show up too often and are hard to get rid of. The reasons are widely documented. We're not nearly as active as we once were. There is precious little fence mending, wood chopping, or cattle herding on the agenda, and if it weren't for former president George W. Bush's vacations in Texas, I suspect our national "brush clearing" tally would be way down too.

Simultaneously, we're spending more time scarfing up treats. As much as we may talk about eating healthier, many homes and offices have a ready supply of cookies, candies, and other sweets rolling through them. *"Mindy's taking another job? That's a shame. What time are we having the cake?"*

In 2010, candy makers used almost 2.5 billion pounds of sugar. That was more than the year before, which was more than the year before that, and so on. And even as we expand our intake, we're not doing much to offset the impact.

In 1960, Americans were an inch shorter than they are now. I mean average Americans, of course—I was only a year old in 1960, so I am much taller now. This gradual increase in height may partly explain our obsession with basketball and why all your grandpa's ties are too short, but it does not explain how our average weight has jumped by twenty-five pounds.

The human head weighs around ten pounds, and on a regular human it's about twelve inches in height. (I chose the mathematically indistinct term *regular*, because as long as celebrities and TV anchors are around, giant craniums will be tilting the numbers.) So each inch of head weighs about four-fifths of a pound. You see where I am going here? If all twenty-five of those pounds we've picked up since 1960 were packed into that one extra inch of height, we'd look like we were walking around with manhole covers for hats. That would be entertaining, but in truth we have distributed those extra pounds all over our staggering frames. A shade more than three-quarters of us are overweight, and a substantial number are obese.

I still remember discovering how my weight had crept up when I wasn't running or exercising at all. Ronnie had started high school, and Ali was still in middle school. I hadn't perched atop a bathroom scale in some years, but only because we didn't own one. Then Linda bought a scale and plopped it on the floor, and I hopped on to see how it worked.

"Hmmm," I muttered. I stepped off and back on. "Hmmm," I repeated.

"Something wrong?" Linda asked from the other side of the bathroom.

"I think your new scale is broken."

"Why?"

"It's way off. Do you know how to adjust it?"

"It's digital. There is no 'adjusting.' Unless you mean adjusting to what it says."

"It can't be right," I said, frowning.

"What can't be right?" Ali and Ronnie had appeared in the doorway.

"This scale says I'm at least ten pounds heavier than I am."

"Ten?" Linda said.

"All right, fifteen. But it's wrong no matter what it says."

"You know, Dad," Ali said, "you're not very active. We've been studying this in school, and people who work in offices often think they are busy because they drive a lot, and they walk to the copy machine, and they go to meetings, but actually they're barely moving all day."

"Then why am I so tired in the evening?"

"That's stress, not fatigue," Ronnie pitched in. "And by the way, if you worked out a little, that stress would ease up."

It was a wake-up call. My build is such that the extra weight did not show much, and like most people, I assumed when a piece of clothing was unusually snug that something had gone awry at the dry cleaners. Or perhaps that Linda was secretly having my suits altered to gaslight me and set up a strong case for divorce on grounds of mental incompetence. I had no real suspicion that she wanted out of the marriage, but I had no suspicion that I was picking up pounds like a baby beluga either.

The return to running had stopped the weight gain I'd spotted on that fateful day. Ultrarunning, however, was pushing the process into reverse.

The math tells the story. When a 200-pound man runs a couple of hours at a moderate clip (say 9- to 10-minute miles), he'll burn around 1,800 calories. The same guy sitting at a desk could get through the whole day on that many calories. When you start running considerably more than two hours in a day, day after day, week after week, your body turns into a biofuel furnace. Whatever you throw in is devoured by your energy-starved system. Pizza, cookies, candy, doughnuts, hamburgers—it seems to make no difference what you consume or how much of it. It's like being twelve years old, but with stiffer joints and a mortgage.

Note that I said "seems to make no difference." Sure, I could quickly process just about anything, including those greasy chicken wings that my wife was worried about, but that did not make it a good idea. Training was forcing me to think more critically about what I was eating, because I needed so much fuel that I didn't want to waste time on foods that wouldn't help me. I could feel the difference. Eat a load of fast sugars or typically "bad" foods and the impact was undeniable. The meal would set me up for a hot start with my body twitching to burn off the burst of junk energy, but it wouldn't last.

After five or six miles, the tank would be running low. By eight or nine, my legs would start going flat. By thirteen or fourteen, I would feel as if I were hauling the week's trash behind me to some distant curb for pickup.

By comparison, if I took in plenty of clean proteins and other foods to prop up my muscles, things like grilled chicken, vegetables, and fruits, I could enjoy a slower distribution of the energy. Instead of hitting the trail like I was on fire, I'd experience an easier buildup to a solid, sustainable pace, and often not crash at all, even though I might run twenty miles or more.

Just as I had with my liquids, I experimented with foods, sorting out which ones worked best before, during, and after a run. In ultramarathons, even as the body demands more fuel, the digestive system becomes persnickety. Runners must come up with plans for eating that revolve around foods that will give them power and yet can also be tolerated by their severely stressed stomachs and intestines.

I tried bagels and bananas, peanut butter and power bars, hamburgers and half-smoked sausages. While I did not hit on a perfect formula, I began developing a sense of what worked and what made me feel bad.

"Remember," Ronnie told me, "don't eat, drink, or do anything wildly different on race day from what you did during training. The race will be a big enough shock."

"Good advice," I told her. "Where'd you hear that?"

"From you."

It was true, and not just for running. I'd often cautioned the girls to seek as much normalcy as possible when tackling any great challenge. Before a big test, a job interview, or even a long trip, I advised them to sleep, eat, and exercise like usual to promote calm, clear thoughts.

"Thanks for the reminder," I told her.

Throughout all this, I also learned to live with a considerably higher level of risk than I had ever accepted in running before. Scratches, bee stings, and bloody spots from one ankle crashing against the other were common. Falls were a constant, and even though I grew better at tucking and rolling—with my water bottles flying in all directions—there were plenty of days when I finished with blood running from my knees and soaking my socks. Given the alternatives, I was grateful. I jerked my head to escape unseen branches trying to smack out my teeth, I jumped over stumps that materialized from the mud to split my shins, and in some spots I ran at full stride, balancing along rock ledges where a misstep could end in a skull-crushing fall.

And still the mileage mounted.

SIXTEEN

One morning, after I'd stood in a freezing shower to reduce the swelling in my legs, taped up my wounds, and started getting dressed for work, Linda asked, "What is a short run these days?"

"Twelve miles or so," I replied.

"Or so?"

"More like fourteen."

It was just a question, and she said nothing more, but I could see the caution light blinking over her head. She was patient and encouraging, but I could tell that running was becoming a sore point. For months she'd not only endured my extended absences but also tolerated incessant talk about running, paces, shoes, and diets. Running magazines were strewn all over the house, the washer and dryer were constantly filled with gear, and our home e-mail was being inundated with race spam. She'd started making up excuses when family members called, rather than saying for the umpteenth time, "No, he's not here. He's running." It was like she was hiding a secret addiction that had claimed her husband, and in a way that was true.

"You should be paying more attention to her," Ronnie told me on the phone. She was back at Georgia Tech and neck-deep in her studies. "That training takes a lot of time."

"I know."

"I'm not sure you do. See, I haven't been running nearly as much since I completed the marathon, and it's made me aware of just how much time I was out there. I mean, work here is always tough, but I feel like I have oceans of time compared with last winter. That's another thing I got out of the race. I manage time much better now."

"Has Mom said anything to you about my training?"

"Only a little."

"Like what?"

"Like, 'Ronnie, I can't believe you got him back into this. What the hell were you thinking?'"

"She said that?"

"Not in so many words, but that's what the subtitles said."

"That doesn't sound very good."

"I'm just telling you that she's trying to be patient and encouraging, and you need to make sure you don't take it for granted."

Easier said than done. With Stone Mill growing closer, my habit was getting worse. I would participate in the Parks Half Marathon in a week as a training run, adding six miles at the end to record nineteen miles for the day. I had signed up for the Marine Corps Marathon as my last big run before Stone Mill, and I was threatening to run from home to the start line, tacking on an additional seven miles. Saturday mornings were filled with running. So were Sundays. I was now routinely going out for runs that lasted from three to five hours. When I wasn't on the trail or at work, I was exhausted.

And it wasn't just Linda who could use some more attention. Ali was once again busy with high school. I flopped down next to her late one evening, barely able to keep my eyes open.

"How's it going, Tiger?" I asked.

"It's going," she said with a frown, dropping a pencil into the book on her lap. "Can you answer a question? And be straight with me. Am I ever going to actually use any of the things I'm learning in calculus?"

"No. Not unless you become, you know, like a physicist or mathematician."

"That's not going to happen. So, if I become an interior decorator, or a car salesman, or a meeting planner, or the CEO of Coca-Cola, I won't need this?"

"You left out stripper."

"Or that."

"No. You will never use calculus. Ever."

"Then why am I learning it?"

"Because you have to. Because it is part of the process. Because it is like training. You do the miles because they harden you for the challenges ahead. You do calculus, and you study Shakespeare, and you read history, and you learn chemistry, because it all trains your brain. It makes you better prepared to take on difficulties, no matter what you decide to do with your life."

"So, even if I become a stripper, I'll be better at figuring out how to split the tips with the other girls."

"Now you're learning. Other than that, is everything good with you?"

"Yep," she said. She pushed the book aside and moved up closer, taking my hand to drape my arm over her shoulders. I knew from Linda that Ali had been frustrated by some friends, and one particular teacher was driving her crazy, but I also knew that this was her way of communicating. She was smart enough to need little direct advice about her problems, but vulnerable enough to need—as we all do—small moments of reassurance, in which she knew she was loved and looked out for. She hadn't been getting enough of that from me, and I pulled her close, soaking up the moment.

"I like that," she said.

"The cuddling?" I asked.

"No. When you call me Tiger."

Part of me was worried that this quest was turning into the exact opposite of what I had hoped. While running was helping me build a new bond with Ronnie, I feared it was becoming a wedge between me and the rest of the family. Even Nola, our sheltie, seemed to cast disappointed eyes at me when I was too tired to play.

Yet I could not imagine quitting, and I told myself it was just for a short while longer. The only plan I could come up with was to make a little breathing space. I cleared out a Friday evening and took Linda to a favorite haunt, a relaxed sports bar with a friendly staff and comfortable booths. We ordered a chicken quesadilla and chatted about work and the kids. I coaxed her into some fried pickles and a margarita. We looked over the movie schedule to see if we might take in a late show. We laughed. We flirted. She ordered coffee, and I ordered a brownie with ice cream. We kept on talking about the kids, the house, plans for the upcoming albeit still-distant holidays, and vacation ideas for the next year. We got into a long thread about hybrid cars and about whether we were due to replace our automobiles anytime soon. We reminisced about our dating days. The bill came, and still we lingered. By the time I looked at my watch, a shade over two hours had passed in which the rigors of running and its endless demands seemed far away, outside the magical, intimate bubble of conversation and touching fingertips. I felt relaxed and happy. She looked that way as well. Perhaps I was too relaxed, because without thinking, I popped a question.

"How do you feel about headlamps?"

"Pardon?" she said, blinking.

My eyes widened at my own callous mistake. "Umm . . ."

"Pardon?" she repeated.

I was in it. No point in turning back. "Umm, I need a headlamp."

She stared at me.

"For running," I added.

"I assumed," she said, sighing and looking at the table and the shards of the broken spell. "Why?"

"Because the days are getting shorter, my mileage has to get longer, and pretty soon I'll be starting my morning runs in the dark."

"Your mileage is already insanely long." Her voice rose. "There are people who commute into D.C. every day who drive fewer miles in a week than you run in a day. And you're already starting in the dark."

"I mean serious dark." So far my most ambitious morning

runs had been on the edge of dawn. "Plus I have to start Stone Mill in the dark, and the race director requires every runner to have a light."

"Then maybe you ought to ask that race director to join you for the next date! I can't believe you. Let's go!" she said, rising abruptly from the booth.

I'd gone too far. After a perfectly wonderful, restorative evening, the great running fight I had feared was finally at hand, and I could not blame her. I stood to follow her to the car, where it would surely erupt in full. She yanked on her jacket, snatched up her purse, and turned for the door. Then she paused. Her shoulders relaxed again. She rotated back to face me with a weary look, sadness and fatigue etched around her eyes. I thought she might cry. Instead, after a long moment, the smallest smile appeared, as if she'd just considered the ridiculousness of what I'd said and the magnificent absurdity of what I was attempting. "Let's go to the movie tonight and have some fun," she said. "We can get your headlamp tomorrow."

True to her word, the next morning she drove with me to our local REI, where we were soon looking over racks of shiny new, lightweight hiking/climbing/running lights with adjustable beams. The salesman, an outdoorsy twentysomething named Scott, seemed impressed about the race as he walked us through the options.

"Now, this one," he said, "gives a nice wide beam, but I'm not crazy about its reach. Will you be running a lot of hills?"

"So I'm told."

"Then this is not for you. Not nearly enough definition. Here's one with self-adjusting intensity."

"Sounds like my college girlfriend," I said.

He didn't laugh. Linda yawned.

"How about rain? Expecting much of that?" he said.

"Maybe. Could get some snow. More likely it will just be cold."

"Then you'll need extra battery strength. The cold will really sap your power. How do you feel about lithium ion?"

After a half hour, during which Linda rolled her eyes so often that I thought she was having a seizure, I picked out one based on the color of the headband and we were on our way. I wore it around the house that evening, frightening the dog and annoying the girls with impromptu scenes from *Marathon Man*. I'd slip up on them as they watched TV or chatted in the kitchen, flick on my light, and say, "Is it safe?"

Up until this point, I'd restricted my early runs to reasonably well-lit roads. On the longest routes, I'd looped up through Bethesda, down past the National Zoo, and into Georgetown, scooting through the glow of streetlamps before grinding home.

With the headlamp, for the first time I could venture onto my remote woodland trails while the sun was still snoozing. The next morning I rose shortly after four to give it a try. Dropping down from my neighborhood, I traced the canal path for a while, then stepped into the woods, pushed toward the river, and entered a fantasy world. Thick fog billowed, making phantoms of the trees even as my headlamp tried to cut the gloom. The sound of my steps and breathing seemed preternaturally loud, as did each chirp of a cricket or croak of a frog. Water burbled invisibly nearby. Every now and then, a sleeping bird would burst from the brush with a squawk and a flutter.

My light danced over the trail, making every rock, root, and undulation leap from the darkness. Getting accustomed to that view took some adjustment. I found myself either over- or underestimating the distance to obstacles and tripping repeatedly. I manipulated the beam to get just the right range and width. As I came over a ridge, I flicked it upward to show more distance, and a buck reared steps away. His hooves cut the air, his antlers raked the darkness, and he was gone, leaving me with my thundering heart.

By the time the sun appeared almost two hours later, I was exhausted but getting the hang of it. I had agreed to meet Linda and Ali at an orchard to pick apples. I calculated the distance at twenty-two miles, and I happily pushed in their direction.

In the days before the raging popularity of GPS watches especially, trail running was an inexact science. The days in which I set out to run a seven-mile trail only to find that it was ten miles long are too numerous to recount. Some of it has to do with the trails themselves being rambling, harum-scarum mazes of dirt, rocks, and weeds, sometimes shaped by humans, sometimes by animals, sometimes by unseen forces like floods and fire. Accurately estimating distances is difficult at best when the path goes up, down, and around countless times. On top of that, fallen trees, washed-out ravines, and rock slides constantly force changes of plan. The trail you run today will not necessarily be the same trail tomorrow.

I had been vaguely aware of this, but as I headed down a country road toward the orchard, I was given a cruel reminder. I had just watched a couple of bow hunters emerge in heavy camouflage from the woods, grateful that they had not mistaken me for a deer, when I saw an orange sign a quarter mile ahead. I ran to it, read the words "Bridge Out," and kept going anyway. I figured at worst I'd have to pick my way over a few stones to ford the stream and then continue on my way. That was a mistake. The bridge was not damaged; it was gone. The creek was deep, rushing, cold, and so hemmed by brush that I knew my plan would not work. I had no choice but to double back and find another way to the orchard.

Getting lost in a car is relatively benign. It is irritating, but, given time and some help, you'll always wind up back in civilization. This was more like getting lost while simultaneously running out of gas.

I had been so confident in my plan that I had consumed the last of my water twenty minutes earlier. The power bar I'd shoved into my belt when I'd left the house was history. I was in the middle of nowhere and going nowhere fast. Minute after minute passed while I trudged down country roads, guessing which one might take me to the right place.

By the time I spotted the orchard over a rise and I cut overland to reach it, my tongue was hanging to my knees.

"Water, water," I said to Linda and Ali, who looked fresh and relaxed as they tumbled from the car.

"Sure," Ali said, handing over a bottle. "And where were you? We've been waiting thirty minutes."

I would later add up the distance I'd covered. It was about twenty-eight miles. More than a full marathon. This was the longest distance I had ever run at one stretch and my first unofficial ultra.

Still, the mileage grew. Within two more weeks, I was running the equivalent of a marathon every Saturday, and another one every Sunday. I would rest on Mondays and Fridays, but mid-week the punishment continued. I would tack on at least thirty-five miles from Tuesday through Thursday, and sometimes more. Most training weeks were pushing eighty miles of running. Some were closer to ninety.

Linda eyeballed the striations in my legs, the muscles upon muscles hardened by the nonstop punishment.

"Man," she said, "your bumps have bumps now."

SEVENTEEN

The Parks Half Marathon is a delightful, point-to-point race that starts in a distant suburb of D.C., winds through tree-covered asphalt trails, and ends up in Bethesda, not far from where I live. Even when I was barely running, I would make it out to the Parks each September.

Linda would always arise with me and drive toward the starting line in Rockville, Maryland. We would grab coffee, a cinnamon roll, and a Diet Coke on the way, and then I'd hop out to join the crowd of runners while she drove back home to sleep another hour before heading to the finish to cheer me on. This year, however, she was heading home to pick up Ali, and they were going to see the grandparents in New Jersey.

"Are you certain you don't need me to give you a ride when you're done?" she asked as I stepped out of the car.

"No, no, no. You've seen my mileage. This will be a piece of cake."

"That's what has me worried. You've been stacking up so many miles that I'm wondering if you're going to crash and burn. Be careful."

"I'm ready to rumble. See you later tonight. Drive safely!"

I fell in with the stream of others trotting to the starting line on a narrow road beneath a Metro train overpass. The crowd is always friendly at this race, and I nodded to everyone who looked even slightly familiar.

I felt stronger than I ever had before. My absurd level of training had reduced the idea of a half marathon to nothing, and I was eager to start. The waves of faster runners started releasing. I positioned myself well back in the corrals, just as I had in Atlanta with Ronnie, to avoid being sucked into the vortex too swiftly.

"How's it going?" I asked a nervous-looking young guy in a bright blue top as we awaited our start.

"Great," he said, as if he did not believe it. "It's my first half marathon."

"You look good," I told him. "Like you're ready for it."

"Oh yeah," he said. "I've been training hard."

This is a typical exchange near the back of the pack, and I was sympathetic to his jitters. As your miles soar, it's easy to forget what a huge accomplishment three, six, or ten miles can be to a new runner and how a half marathon can seem as inaccessible as the moon. Yet here I was, among men and women who were jumbles of nerves, and it's almost a religious tenet of running that better runners encourage others along.

"Like I said," I repeated to the kid as our wave made it to the starting mat, "you look great. What's your name?"

"Brad. I'm from Alexandria."

I could barely hear him over an announcer at the line bellowing through a loudspeaker. It would be worth the effort just to run away from that noise.

"I'm Tom. I'm from here. See you at the finish line!"

And our wave was off and running.

The first couple of miles were on a wide-open thoroughfare with slightly rolling hills. Some of the runners were already bitching over the elevation changes, but after all I'd been through, it felt like nothing. By the time we turned into the woods, which made up most of the course, I was settling into a smooth rhythm.

The hills came quicker now, and the trail was tighter, but my stride stayed solid. I would pick out a runner of similar speed and tuck in behind him, drafting as he cut the humid air. After a while, I would pull out, pass, and start hunting down my next windbreaker. It is an effective way to run if you can pull it off. You conserve energy while simultaneously pushing yourself to keep the pace, and on this morning, it was working like a charm.

Eventually I wound up alongside a guy a little younger, who kept slipping sidelong glances.

"How's it going?" he said. "You're the guy on the news, aren't you?"

"Yes, I'm Tom."

"Daniel. I'm from Baltimore."

This happens from time to time during races. People recognize me from CNN and want to say hi or discuss the news. Some folks in highly public jobs dislike being spotted in their off-time. I've never minded, and I try to take a few moments. In any event, I backed off to visit and save my legs for the end.

We talked for a few miles about the morning, the crowd, the racecourse, and other races we'd run. He'd done the Baltimore Marathon and thought it was terrific. I told him I would take on the Marine Corps Marathon in a few weeks.

"Now that's a great race," he said. "Big crowds, wonderful support, and the medal is nice."

"I'm looking forward to it," I said. It was pleasant enough, but soon I had rested plenty and I started stepping up the pace. At first it was nearly imperceptible, but after a half mile Daniel was sucking air.

"I think you better go on without me," he said. It is the protocol of runners. Don't make someone ask to leave you. If you can't keep up, let them go with your blessing.

"Thanks, pal," I said. "Nice running with you. See you later."

We were in the final four miles and my time was looking better than ever before for the Parks. My speed was increasing, and I still felt as if I'd just started. Sweeping into the long straightaway to the finish, I was flying.

The final section cut through a tunnel. I emerged to a cheering crowd and the finish line ahead. I did not slow a step. The race had never been easier. I blew through the finish, ate a banana in the recovery tent, and with my number still flapping, I started the six miles home. On the way, I met another couple also running with their race numbers. We were so far from the course that we all knew that we were stacking up serious miles. The young woman looked my way and raised her fist.

"Yay, overachievers!" she shouted.

I waved back. Damn right.

A couple of weeks later, I flew to Atlanta to see my own overachiever. Ronnie had already told me about her reduced running schedule, but she was still cranking down a few miles.

Her classes in the aerospace department, arguably the best in the world, demanded extraordinary amounts of discipline and time, and she had found that running kept her energy up and her mind sharp. She had asked me to come down for an October half marathon as I hit the home stretch to Stone Mill.

"How did you find time to do this?" I asked as we took off with a few thousand runners, working our way through a northern suburb. The morning was cold and clear, the crowd happy.

"I've been much better at prioritizing things ever since the marathon, and I don't just mean schoolwork. Everything. I don't throw away time anymore. If I really want to do something, I find a way to fit it in. How about you?"

"Work has been a bear lately. Seems like I'm juggling multiple stories every day. Ali's homework is keeping her busy. Your mom is tending to a million different things, as usual. And of course, my mileage is off the hook." She listened as I recounted all the trails and roads and talked about running in the dark and rain. I carried on about sports drinks, energy bars, blisters, shoes, and the cycle of fatigue and recovery.

"That's great," she said after a while, "but what about everything else? I mean, I'm working hard down here, but I'm still making time for my friends. We've gone hiking. I've been to the beach. We go out for brunch. I don't have time for much outside my studies, but I fit in some other things because I think I need to. You still have to do things for fun."

Her words brought to mind a disquieting fact: I had reached the point where I'd given up almost everything except running. I could scarcely recall the last time I'd sat at the piano, although both girls had warm childhood memories of falling asleep as I played far into the night. My guitars were collecting dust, and no doubt hideously out of tune. I touched my left thumb against my fingertips and found them soft, no longer firm and ready to push the strings against the frets as they had been for thirty years. My art supplies sat unused in the closet, and it had been months since Linda had found one of my drawings absently left on the coffee table. I used to do them all the time: little pictures of the dog, or her, or a plant, or a banana. Reading had been the most persistent passion of my life. As a boy in Illinois, I pedaled my bicycle three miles to the town library to check out books, and I was so eager to plunge into them that on the straight farm roads home I would ride with no hands, reading in transit. I had not glanced at my bedside stack of books in weeks.

I had made a conscious decision that running would trump every other hobby or pastime until Stone Mill was done. Ronnie's comments, however, reminded me of how much I was giving up. And how much I missed it.

"You know," she said, "there is such a thing as pushing too hard. You can go a lot farther than you think sometimes, but there are still limits. We're studying that in one of my classes. See, you can put the biggest engine you want into a rocket, but if the rest of the spacecraft can't handle all that energy, it's going to blow to pieces. You've got to have balance. I realized after I finished the marathon that running one is not so tough. Doing it without letting the rest of your life fall apart is the challenge."

This is a thought that is often overlooked in all the inspirational running books and websites. Plenty of writers talk about mind over matter and about runners "willing" themselves to the finish line, but precious few address the possibility that maybe doggedly chasing a goal is not enough. We ran on through manicured neighborhoods where people stood in their robes watching with beagles on leashes and newspapers under their arms.

"You know," I said after a while, "I'm still barely covering enough training distance for the race."

"Really?"

"Yeah. I'm sort of at the minimum level for even attempting a race like this, and I'm nervous about it."

"Being nervous is okay," she said. "That's something else I learned. After all, what's the worst thing that can happen?"

"I could keel over, roll into a stream, be washed out into the Atlantic, and never be heard from again."

"So, would you be leaving a big inheritance for me and Ali?"

"Not so much."

"How about just for me?"

"No, not even that much."

"Then that would be tragic." She smiled. "Anyway, I'm sure you'll work it all out."

I knew now that she was talking about a lot more than running, and I wondered if this was really why she wanted me to come to Atlanta. In any event, we loosened up then and joked our way through the rest of the run, soaking up the warming sun and the scenery. I thought about how much I enjoyed being with her. After we collected our medals and performed our ceremonial swap, we hopped in the rental car and made our way back to Georgia Tech. I grabbed my things for the airport.

"Listen, Dad," Ronnie said at the car window, "just do your

best and have fun. You have prepared for this as much as you can under the circumstances of your life. Mom, Ali, and I all know how hard you've worked for this and what it means to you. Whether you finish or not, enjoy the journey. We'll be with you every step."

We hugged, I drove away, and shortly I was winging over the Eastern Seaboard back to D.C. with only a couple of tests remaining before what I imagined would be the race—or wreck—of a lifetime.

EIGHTEEN

*T*he Marine Corps Marathon is one of those mega-marathons that draws national attention and thirty thousand weekend warriors, and, on this last chilly Sunday morning in October, my friend Ted Fine. Ted is a producer with Bloomberg in New York whose company I've always enjoyed, so I was delighted when he suggested we run the MCM together. Now, as we made our way to the starting line in a rock concert pack of others, everywhere I looked I saw new shoes.

"Seems like a lot of first-timers," I said. A howitzer boomed over our heads—part of the atmosphere the Semper Fi gang brings to the festivities.

"Looks that way," Ted responded. "It's good of them to be out here."

Ted is one of the most understanding, encouraging, and natural athletes I know. He plays hockey, golf, and basketball and runs as effortlessly as most people breathe. Some years ago, when he was with CNN, we were sent to Boulder for yet another follow-up on the JonBenét Ramsey murder case, and we ran together for the first time. Ted had previously lived there, and he had a favorite trail. We started at the base of a small hill and soon were thundering up an honest-to-God, western, rip-your-lungs-out-and-feed-them-back-to-you mountain. Ted moved as effortlessly as a goat, while I blew like a steam engine. I grabbed rock outcroppings, braced myself on pine trees, and wheezed through tight spots, as Ted bounded along with gravity-defying grace. When I reached the top, twenty minutes later, my hair was splayed in all directions, my eyes were blinking through rivers of sweat, and my lungs were all but cracking my ribs as I siphoned oxygen from the mile-high air.

"Can you slow down a little?" Ted asked, cruising to the summit behind me with his forehead barely damp. "I can hardly keep up with you."

He wasn't being sarcastic. He's just that athletically gifted and gracious. Before the Marine Corps Marathon, Ted had told me on the phone that he hadn't run much at all. I'd replied, "No problem. It will be my final long training run before Stone Mill, so I'll just take it easy and run with you."

As we maneuvered to the starting line, I had no inkling how soon I would regret my words of largess. We made a quick stop at the Porta-Johns, and I jumped into a short line only to realize why it was short. My shoes sank into a mire of wet grass and mud, which soaked my socks. Not an auspicious beginning. I shook off the muck, and we slipped into a starting corral to await the gun.

Many first-timers believe that, on the basis of its name, the Marine Corps Marathon is a particularly difficult race, as if they'll have to run it under heavy cannon fire or with a drill sergeant yelling at them the whole way. To the contrary, it is easy, as marathons go. The course is rolling to flat, the scenery is appealing, and the support is excellent. Large crowds turn out to wave signs, cheer, and create a festive air. Parachutists drop from the sky, and iconic warplanes buzz overhead. It starts and ends in Virginia close by the famed Iwo Jima Memorial, where four bronze Marines are forever raising a flag across the river from the D.C. skyline. Many volunteers are members of the military, and they hand out cold water with cheerful efficiency. The swag is also great: free samples galore, Marine patches, bumper stickers, bandanas, and shirts emblazoned with a carnival of patriotic emblems. Scads of military folks run, some in combat boots and uniforms. And little known to those who run in D.C., when the start is sounded, Marines stationed all over the world take off to simultaneously run their own marathons in far-flung places in a program called MCM Forward. If you want inspiration, this is a race that brings it.

The biggest challenge is its popularity. Started back in 1976 as a way of rebuilding relations between the military and civilians after the Vietnam War, it was an instant hit, and it more than doubled in size in its second year. Steadily expanding ever since, it has earned its nickname, "the People's Marathon." From start to finish, runners must maneuver in close proximity to each other and the crowd, with a few bottlenecks funneling everyone into an elbow-to-elbow squeeze.

None of that was a problem for Ted and me, since we weren't looking to set any records. We fell into the rhythm of the pack as the race began, jogging amid cheery blasts of frozen breath, talking about our families, sports, work, and movies.

"Look at that!" Ted said, as a young guy burned past wearing Roman-style sandals laced up his calves.

"I don't care what kind of shape you're in," I said. "That can't be easy."

A few of the bridges were slick with frost, and we'd both started the race wearing leggings against the biting cold, but by mile 7 we were warm. After churning up a mild hill, we pulled them off, tied them to a tree for later retrieval, and headed into Georgetown.

The sight of the crowd was downright shocking, compared with the wooded emptiness in which I'd been training. Cheering people lined K Street as it cut through the popular shopping district, past tony boutiques, by places with four-dollar coffees, and in front of the historic house where George Washington helped lay out the capital's road map. The number of spectators diminished as we moved down by the river, passing the old Watergate Hotel and the Kennedy Center, and then built again, sizably and rapidly, as we came up behind the Lincoln Memorial.

Volunteers shouted as we approached aid stations.

"Water, water, water!"

"Gatorade, Gatorade, Gatorade!"

We grabbed cups, gulped them down, and kept going. I was wearing my bottle belt as much for practice as for anything else, since I need to be fully accustomed to the weight. I also had my phone jammed into a pocket, and I pulled it out to grab a few photos.

"This is really nice," Ted said. "I love all the kids."

The course was lined with families there to cheer on dads, moms, brothers, and sisters. Ted started high-fiving children who held up their hands, and I was thinking, once again, how smart I was to slow down and enjoy my time with him. Then

I noticed something. Ted was gaining speed. At first I thought I was mistaken, but a check of my watch showed our mile splits were dropping.

Having established weeks earlier that I was the fit one, and Ted the straggler whom I was graciously assisting, I could not very well ask him to slow down. I'd been running the equivalent of more than three marathons a week for a month and a half. Certainly, this had to be a burst of unexpected enthusiasm, and he would soon calm down. Or so I told myself.

I dropped a half step back and hung on as we boiled out to Hains Point, cut back past the Jefferson Memorial, and wound around by the new Martin Luther King, Jr. Memorial. The crowd was growing denser, and Ted was having a ball—and going even faster. He spotted a young woman running in football shoulder pads and a helmet.

"That must be hard," he said to her, laughing.

"It's not that bad," she said. "Just a little tight around the arms!"

"Ha!" Ted said. They talked, as I grunted and dug deep to keep up. It was getting absurd. The more I struggled, the faster Ted went. Images of me burning out entirely in the next five miles and seeing all my ultra dreams go up in smoke were haunting me. I had to act.

"Hey, Ted," I called out as we dodged around fans waving signs and other runners near the Smithsonian's National Museum of Natural History, "are you doing okay? I want to make sure you don't push yourself too hard." My eyes were exploding from their sockets and my legs were aflame, but I tossed the question as if it had just occurred to me.

"I'm feeling fine! This is so much fun."

Dammit. Just what I was afraid of. "Great. It's just that our splits are pretty short. Thought I'd let you know."

"Really? I hadn't noticed. How are they looking?"

I feigned minor interest as I looked at my watch. From easy ten-minute miles, we'd dropped dramatically. I wanted to scream, *"For the love of God, slow down!"* Instead, I casually said, "Pretty fast. We're nearly at eights now. Maybe we should back off a little. We don't want all the fun to be over too soon. What do you think?"

It was all I could do to get the sentence out without fainting.

"Sure. Let's take a couple of pictures," he said.

I looked up and saw that we were right in front of the Capitol. It was majestic and glowing in the morning light. With the applause, the river of runners, and, mercifully, a moment to catch my breath, it was truly lovely. Ted handed his phone to a woman who snapped a couple of pictures of us. I asked her to take a few more, not because I wanted them, but because I needed every possible second to recover. I was about to ask for one more when Ted thanked her, grabbed the camera, and bolted. How I held on for the next three miles I don't know, but when we crossed back over the Potomac into Virginia around mile 21 and the crowd faded, Ted finally turned off the afterburners.

"I didn't realize this was such a wonderful race," he said, beaming like a ten-year-old. His joy was infectious. Or maybe I was developing croup. In any case, through violent coughs and gasps, I said, "It's a good run, all right."

We passed a woman in a lawn chair holding a sign that said "Worst Parade Ever." We both laughed. We saw a guy playing the French horn. We applauded. In the final miles, we ran into a few friends and exchanged hellos, and then we wound around the Pentagon, pressing toward the finish.

The course grew narrower, squeezing the field into a tight stream as we turned up a final hill. Ted accelerated once again, and I held on with everything I had left, fighting the urge to celebrate by vomiting. We crossed the line, and a tall Marine shook our hands and gave us our medals.

We walked a couple of miles out of the melee so that Linda could pick us up, retrieved our leggings from the tree near Georgetown, and went to lunch. Ted was happy. I was too, even though the race had revealed a troubling level of fatigue in my muscles from all my weeks of hard training. When we drove him to the train station later that afternoon, he hugged Linda and shook my hand.

"Best of luck with the big run, buddy," he said, and I knew he meant it.

What I didn't know was how much or how soon I would need that luck.

NINETEEN

The yellow marks on my training calendar nearly covered the page, but I was studying the Stone Mill course map with unease. The Marine Corps Marathon had left a nagging worry. While I wished my mileage was higher, I remained surprised at how my legs suffered chronic lassitude. I continued knocking off massive training runs, and most of the time they felt fine. But at alarmingly regular intervals, exhaustion appeared out of nowhere.

In addition, the fall days were colder than expected, so I habitually prowled the Stone Mill website and discussion pages, noting every hint, every warning, and every clue that might help me survive the course and the conditions. I printed the elevation map and meticulously compared it with Google Earth images. I memorized landmarks and spent hours going through variations of split times to figure out when I might hope to be where.

"Are those from the race?" Ali asked, joining me on the sofa and settling her head on my shoulder. On my laptop, photos from last year's race scrolled past: vacant-eyed runners stumbling into aid stations, wading through knee-deep creeks, and nursing bloody wounds. Some images showed people staggering up slopes that it hurt to imagine in such a long race. Others showed faces in frozen grimaces. Some were smiling as if they were having the time of their lives. I assumed they were delirious.

"This doesn't look so good, Dad," Ali said.

I thought about her perspective. Sitting amid the loving sounds and sights of home, with Linda puttering around in the kitchen and Nola asleep by the fireplace, it seemed ridiculous to plunge into such lunacy.

"I was thinking the same thing," I said. "After all, I could spend that Saturday here with you and Mom. We could go to a movie. Maybe I should back out."

Ali flicked an eye my way and knew I was at least half kidding. She didn't miss a beat. "I don't think so. If you drop out, you'll feel better for a few minutes or maybe an hour, but then you'll wonder what you missed. You'll think about all the hours you put into it and how many hopes you had. You'll think about all the people who have cheered you on and how disappointed they'll be, and you'll regret quitting. Maybe not today, maybe not tomorrow, but soon and for the rest of your life."

"*Casablanca?*"

"It's all I could come up with. Everyone wants to quit when things get hard. It is a measure of your character that you overcome that feeling and fulfill the commitment you made, not to others but to yourself."

"Wow," I said. "What a great little speech. I guess I'll do it after all. Thank you."

"No problem," she said, getting up to grab a snack. "That's what Mom told me when I wanted to quit ballet."

"But you quit anyway, didn't you?"

"That was me. And for crying out loud, it was ballet. Go run your race."

True athletes are not like the rest of us. Some of us can rise to glorified amateur status by dominating all comers in the Spring Fling tennis tournament, or dropping a twenty-foot jumper in pickup basketball, or by grand-slamming our way to the Greater Waukegan softball championship. But I've been around real athletes, and they are different animals. They run faster, jump higher, and lift more. They outmuscle, outmaneuver, and outrun. They bring an animal cunning, quickness, and power to their games all the time that most of us, if we are lucky, may taste once in a lifetime.

In 2004, the greatest active American marathoner of our age, Meb Keflezighi, won the silver medal at the Olympics in Athens with a brilliant dash of 2:11:29. He won the Boston Marathon in 2014, the first American man to do so in more than thirty years. In 2011, Geoffrey Mutai of Kenya broke the record in Boston with a time of 2:03:02. That's about 4:42 per mile. In 2003, Paula Radcliffe from the United Kingdom scorched the field in the London Marathon with a time of 2:15:25. That's 5:09 a mile. On the best running day of my life, back when I was seventeen, I ran Radcliffe's pace for three miles. It nearly killed me.

A glance at *UltraRunning* magazine's website reveals even more radical numbers. In 2013, Zach Bitter from Wisconsin ran 100 miles in 11:47:21. Russia's Oleg Kharitonov ran the same distance almost 20 minutes faster in 2002. Bruce Fordyce from South Africa ran 50 miles in 4:50:21 in 1984, although he is better known for winning Comrades nine times.

It's hard to refer to these as world or national records, since the courses vary wildly, but the ultra community has its heroes and celebrities: Scott Jurek, Ann Trason, Max King, Dean Karnazes, Mike Morton, and Sabrina Little, to name a few, even if it's hard to measure exceptionalism in a sport where so many events are mind-boggling.

So I have never imagined myself to be an athlete, and for all my confidence, that thought stuck with me as the final days ticked down to Stone Mill. I had covered many miles, I had made training a part of my weekly schedule as surely as breathing, and I was more athletic than I'd ever been before. Still, I did not feel like an athlete.

"Why not?" Ronnie asked on the phone. "You've covered a ton of miles, you train every week, and I've never seen you in better shape."

"I don't know. I guess I just have too much respect for the people who are really good at this to compare myself to them."

"But it's their job," she said. "Listen, I saw an interview on a talk show. The host asked a fashion model what advice she had for women who wanted to look like her. The model said something like, 'They should realize that this is my occupation. I'm paid to work out, to have my hair done, and to have professional makeup artists put me together. Honestly, I am in awe of how other women handle jobs, husbands, children, houses, and everything else while still staying in shape and looking gorgeous. I could never do that as well as they do.'"

"I think I get your point. So you think I'm doing okay?"

"If you're not, we'll still say nice things at the funeral," she said. "Anyway, we'll find out soon enough, won't we?"

The anticipation and anxiety as the race day drew near

made me irritable, jumpy, and excited. Linda and Ali were too close to the madness to be the best sounding boards. I found myself looking forward to Ronnie's daily pep talks as a stabilizing force. Her calm and encouraging words pushed me toward the proper equilibrium. So I smiled when I was sitting at my desk and the phone rang that morning. It was a time that she usually called, and I picked it up expecting to hear her voice. Instead, I heard my mother on the line.

"Your brother has had a heart attack."

My head filled with noise. My hands went cold.

"When? How?"

"Last night. He wasn't feeling well all evening, and then he passed out. The ambulance took him . . ."

The rest of the story came in a fog. At the emergency room, they had determined that it was a massive one, a "widow maker," as the doctor put it. They discussed the situation with his wife, Beth, and then plunged a needle into Robert's chest, making an all-or-nothing bid to save him. It worked. He'd been rushed off to a larger medical center an hour and a half away for more treatment. I was told not to call until the next day, after he'd had time to rest. The next twenty-four hours were endless. Finally, after getting an all clear from my sister, Chris, I dialed the hospital.

"Hello?" Robert sounded as if nothing had happened.

"Hey, it's me," I stammered. "How are you doing?"

"I'm fine," he said, although I could hear a trace of fatigue in his laugh. "My head hurts from falling. I guess I hit the corner of the bed frame going down, but other than that, I'm all right."

"Seriously? Did they have to put in a stent, or do you need a bypass, or . . ."

"No. None of that. The doctors have me on all kinds of medication, but they say they really can't find any evidence of damage to my heart. At least not the kind they can fix that way."

"How is that possible?"

"Not sure. One of them said maybe the running built up my heart enough to help fight off the effects. Who knows?"

"What happens now?"

"They're going to do some more tests."

"When are you going home?"

"Honestly, if they'd let me go now, I would. I feel like I could go shingle a roof. And I'm not sure how much it is going to help me to spend another night with nurses waking me up every half hour to take some kind of reading or another. How is your training going?"

Just like that, he turned the corner, as if his health were not worth discussing. We talked about my running, about the weather, and about anything but the fact that he had come so close to dying. He made me laugh with a story about his wife's reaction to him pitching over. We talked about our family's long history of heart ailments. I asked him what the doctors said about his future.

"They say I have to take it easy for a while, until they get all this medicine worked out, and they want to do a bunch of follow-ups to make sure they didn't miss anything. Oh, and there's one more thing: They say I'm finished with marathons. That's it."

I called my mother later that evening, when she'd returned from the hospital. She gave me the latest updates. I mentioned how much he loved running, and she sided with the doctor. "I wish you'd all give it up," she said, "at least all that long running. I worry about you."

Robert agreed that there was no real reason for me to go to Alabama to see him. The immediate danger was past, and by all accounts his life would soon go back to more or less normal. We were heading down for Thanksgiving in a few weeks anyway. Linda and I talked about it into the night. My brother had always been heavier than I was, and his weight had fluctuated over a greater range. He faced a lot of stress in his work, and he held it all in. He seldom ate well, and he had ignored the advice of doctors for as long as I could remember.

"Still, it makes you wonder, doesn't it? I mean, he's tough. If his heart had trouble, couldn't mine?"

"Maybe you should get it checked," she said.

"Maybe."

Ronnie provided the counterbalance.

"I know it has to be scary for you," she said on the phone. "He's your big brother, and you've always looked up to him."

"Yeah. It also makes me think that maybe I'm being foolish. You and Ali count on me to be here. You need me to provide for you, to do things, and to be the dad in this family. Maybe at my age I shouldn't be messing around with all this running. I mean, the marathon was one thing, but this has gotten out of hand. What if I fall out there and get disabled somehow? Or what if I have a heart attack of my own? Where would you be then? What would you do?"

"We would be okay. We would help you," she said. "You haven't raised weak girls. We're strong because you and Mom have taught us to be. Strong enough to do our part if something went wrong. You know how you used to grab my hand when we were little and we went running?"

I hadn't thought of it in years. When she was tiny and we ran somewhere, she would sometimes grow tired, but we would not stop. Instead, she would extend a hand, and I would pull her along using my legs to help her battle gravity, her exhausted legs, and the desire to quit.

"I'm grabbing your hand now," she said. "You can do this. You should do this. You're fine."

TWENTY

For weeks I had been trying to make it out to the Stone
Mill course so that I could see firsthand how it looked.
I'd hoped that my training trails, covered with steep hills
and jagged rocks, had prepared me, but you can learn only so
much from maps. As famed war historian Stephen Ambrose
had told me in an interview years earlier, "If you're going to
understand a battle, at some point you have to walk the ground
where it was waged."

With just one week left before Stone Mill, I made it to the
battlefield. The occasional fatigue in my legs following the
Marine Corps Marathon and all those other runs was fading as
I entered the taper-down phase. My mileage was dwindling so
quickly I was itching to go farther. I knew better. This was not
a time for devouring miles. It was a time for pulling back and
displaying a different kind of discipline. Linda drove me to the
suburban high school where the Stone Mill would start. The
parking lot was empty and the sun shining.

"Here's my plan," I told her. "I'm going to go out for a nice,
easy tour of the first section. I'm not going to run hard. I'm
just going to rest my legs and get a feel for the trail."

"You sound like you're trying to convince yourself."

"I am. I feel like I want to run the whole race right now."

"Not sure I can wait here that long today."

"All right. Then can you pick me up on Darnestown Road over by that Starbucks?"

"That's more like it. Yes, I already have the intersection in the GPS. How long will you take?"

"It's about nine miles, so I figure an hour and a half—tops."

"Okay. Good luck."

I stepped out of the car and pulled off my leggings.

"Those are the whitest legs ever," Linda said. "You ran all summer. How is it possible that you didn't tan at all?"

We laughed, and as she wheeled away, I jogged off toward the woods. It took several minutes to find the Greenway Trail, where the race would commence. It was as narrow as a deer path, and perhaps that should have been a warning. I was confronted with terrain that was considerably different from what I'd expected. The path was cluttered with loose rocks and outcroppings of buried boulders. Roots raked at the toes of my shoes as I slid over stones and crumbling dirt ridges. The path rose and plunged, tilting left, right, forward, and back. The turns rotated as quickly as mountain switchbacks. Leaves covered everything. Placing each step without turning an ankle was a high-stakes guessing game.

Compared with my training runs closer to home, everything here was magnified. The rocks had keener edges and were more numerous. The pitches were steeper. In minutes, my lungs were screaming, my legs were twitching, and sweat was cascading down my face. Worse, I was moving very slowly.

The Spartan slopes and uncertain footing had me working twice as hard to move half as fast.

"Calm down," I said to myself after a couple of miles, speaking aloud to get my own attention. "You're just not used to it. This is a strange course, and it's freaking you out. This is why you're here: to get an idea of what to expect. Everything is going to be fine."

I took deeper breaths and forced myself to look up from the dirt. I wasn't sure where I was. A middle-aged couple on an afternoon hike appeared atop a hill. They smiled as I chugged up.

"Excuse me," I panted, "but this is the Greenway Trail, isn't it?"

"Sure is," said the man, who was paunchy and wearing a Nationals baseball cap. "Out for a run, are you?"

"Training for a race, actually. I just want to make sure that I'm in the right place. I'm heading down to Darnestown Road."

"Heavens!" said the woman, with her bright pink vest and poofy auburn hair. "That's quite a distance. Are you going to run the whole way?"

"I am, but it's not really that far."

Their eyebrows arched.

"How long is the race?" she asked.

"Fifty miles."

"Fifty?" they said in unison.

I smiled weakly and nodded. It was fun to see their surprise, but disconcerting too. They were looking at me as if they were making mental notes so they'd recognize me when the local news covered my disappearance. "Next week there'll be about three hundred runners out here," I said. "We'll go all the way down to the Potomac, then back up by Pennyfield Lock, then . . . well, I'm not sure I can describe all the places we'll go, but it should be a good run."

They wished me luck, and I moved off. I was grateful for the distraction. My heart rate had slowed, and I was calmer, which was useful, because within a few more miles, I was lost. The trail had descended into a winding creek bottom filled with scrub. I'd noticed numerous crude side cuts that could have been erosion or perhaps paths that locals had beaten from their homes into this strip of woods. I'd passed them all with confidence that I knew where I was going, but now the path I'd been following had taken an improbable turn. I was sweeping up a terrible hill, heading in the wrong direction. I doubled back to the creek bottom, looking for clues.

I picked what looked like my best bet and followed it. It wound through the woods and sliced across an open meadow, and that's where I fell the first time. Then it happened again as I went back into the trees. Then again. Then a lot. The apprehension that had started in the wake of the Marine Corps Marathon was erupting inside me. My stomach hurt. My legs felt foreign, wobbling and stumbling as if the earth were alive beneath them. My head was swimming with all the wrong thoughts. I could hardly breathe, and each direction I turned looked exactly like the last one. By the time I broke from the woods, miles from where I started and nowhere near where I expected to be, I felt worse than I had in any race or training run since I began this quest.

It took another ten minutes for me to figure out my location and wind my way over to where Linda was waiting in a parking lot near the designated intersection. She furrowed her brow as

I fell into the passenger seat. "Where have you been? You said that you were going to be here thirty minutes ago, and . . ." Her voice trailed off. Scrutinizing me, she said, "Are you all right?"

"Yes." I paused. "No."

She looked at my dirty hands and scraped knees. I kept my face down so that she wouldn't see the wild look in my eyes.

"You fell?"

"Yes."

"How many times?"

"I lost count."

"Was it rough?"

"You might say that."

I stared out the window while we drove home in silence, except for Linda's last question, which was the one that had haunted me despite all the work, all the races, all the inspirational running books, and all the pep talks: "Are you sure you can do this?"

I thought about the hundreds of miles of training. The cold, the heat, the early mornings and late nights. I saw the rain running down my face and legs, the snow caked on my shoes and shoulders. I thought about the aches, the aspirin, the tape on my toes, the heating pads on my knees, the ice bags on my ankles, and the desperate moments running in strange cities in darkness and uncertainty. I thought about the painstaking way I'd built up for this moment for an entire year. Then I thought about the panic that had been running behind me for the past two hours, nipping at my heels on a course that exceeded my expectations. I felt foolish to have ever imagined, at the age of fifty-one, that this was a race for me.

I thought of all that, and I didn't answer.

TWENTY-ONE

Fingers of light from dozens of headlamps slash the darkness. The air crackles against my skin at 29 degrees. Each time I breathe in, my lungs burn. Each time I breathe out, a dense cloud billows. All around, runners rumble—signing in with the race director, double-checking their supply bags, devouring last-minute power bars, and kissing loved ones goodbye as if we are all about to be launched into the frozen darkness of deep space, perhaps never to be seen again.

Which, as far as I'm concerned, is not far off the mark.

Despite all the training in simulated race conditions and the rituals I followed this morning to brace myself, I feel lost. I know that in a matter of minutes it will be me, the miles, and the elements, and it feels as if nothing I've done has even remotely prepared me for the experience. The week since my practice run has done zero to improve my outlook. I don't belong with these people. I keep thinking of a bumper sticker I saw in the parking lot that said "You ran a marathon? That's cute." To them, it is a joke; to me, it is a threat.

Linda, wearing a heavy coat, gloves, and a fuzzy blue hat, is fussing around me. Despite my fears, I've been trying to convince her that I'm fully recovered and ready to go.

"Are you going to be okay?"

"Sure," I shoot back too quickly and too enthusiastically. "I feel good. Legs strong. Just a little chilly."

"You look hypothermic. And you've only been out of the car for five minutes."

"I'm fine," I say. Or try to say. A sudden tremor whips through me, and it comes out like one of those cartoon characters caught in a deep freeze as "I-I-I-I'm f-f-f-f-f-f-ine . . ."

She gives me her best pharmacist's appraisal. "You could put on your running pants."

"I don't think so. They'll slow me down."

That's not the real reason. Truth be told, with everything else I have working against me, I don't want to advertise my newbie status, and I've already looked the crowd over through my icy eyelashes. While most people are wearing a couple of thin layers of clothing up top, along with hats and gloves, precious few have anything beyond shorts, socks, and shoes from the waist down. In a mere marathon, running pants would be everywhere. Here my headlamp shows red, pink, blue, and purple bare legs all around. It looks like the frozen-chicken section at the grocery store.

This is unlike the start of any other race I've ever seen. Although all 300 slots were snagged by entrants, only about 250 people have shown up. Even though excitement courses through the crowd, it has a different tone. Not a soul here is a casual runner. Not one is scared by big distances. Yet we all know that a substantial number of us will not finish. Accident, injury, fatigue, and despair are hiding in the dark woods. Anyone with doubts is already half beaten, but anyone without them is half crazy.

The race director calls everyone to the start, and the group lurches toward it. Linda stops me long enough to peel off her gloves and take my face between her warm hands. "You have to promise me something. If you get hurt, if you get into trouble, if you get too tired, you have to stop. Promise me."

"I will," I lie.

"Promise."

"I promise," I lie again. Even through my terror, I remain committed to giving it everything I have, come what may.

We hear the "ready" shout. I pose with a heel kicked up and a goofy grin as she grabs a parting photograph. I assume it is for the obituary. I don't even hear the start command; I just see the front-runners lower their heads and move. We all fall in, cutting a swift circle around the school to settle our legs and spread the pack. Then, slipping down a steep grassy slope toward the looming trees and with one last glance back at my wife's waving silhouette, I step into the abyss.

Like many Americans, I was riveted by the saga of those Chilean miners who were trapped underground for sixty-nine days awaiting rescue in 2010, and I was dumbfounded by Edison Peña. He was the manic Elvis fan who kept training for a marathon while sealed in that living tomb, running up to six miles a day while dragging a heavy pallet through the broken tunnels. Less than a month after he emerged from the portal of hell, he took his first airplane ride and ran the New York City Marathon, completing the course in less than six hours despite a knee injury. I often thought of his dedication during my training, and now I wonder if everyone around me might have miners in mind. Perhaps miners on Mars. Our headlamps are flashing over the sharp slopes, casting alien shadows.

The trail, packed with bodies, is narrower than I recall from just a week ago. Rocks and roots leap from under the feet up ahead, repeatedly forcing me into a spastic stutter step to avoid these obstacles. The switchbacks are more devilish in the dark. Leaves blanket everything, blinding me to what lies beneath. Any step can end in a broken toe, a twisted ankle, or a spill that could lead to a DNF or to the hospital, and we've barely started.

The crowd is sorting itself out. The jackrabbits are exploding out front in an early hunt for the lead, the slower runners are staking the back, and most of us are aiming for the middle. The trail is so tight that anyone trying to pass encounters elbows, shoulders, and curses. Most don't attempt it. We keep our eyes on the path, trying to wrap our heads around the merciless miles ahead.

Whenever I dare to look up from the dirt, I see faces of dogged determination and stark fear. I'm clearly not the only one wondering whether this is such a good idea. A guy in a bright red top staggers up next to me as we crest a hill, his knees shaking and sweat washing his face despite the freezing temperature and the fact that we're only two miles in.

"Kind of a rough start, huh?" I ask.

He shoots me a wild-eyed look and yelps, "Burt's my dachshund!" before taking off down the hill. At least that's what it sounds like. Truthfully, I don't know if it is an answer or a cry for help, or if he is leaping right into the cold-induced hysteria that I fully expect to overtake me as the day unwinds. I wonder if I'll see him again. Not that I'm worried about it much. I have my own issues.

After a few miles, the trail drops down by the creek I encountered the week before, and the path flattens. The line strings out, giving us all a little more room, and I settle into a lope to take stock. At the start of every race, experienced runners engage an internal Mission Control to assess how they feel, energy levels, lung capacity, leg strength, the weather, and any unexpected concerns. The situation is not promising.

First, there's the issue of my lungs. I've trained through a lot of cold days. I've run a lot of hills. I've competed in enough races to tamp down some of the chest-tightening adrenaline. But this morning none of that is enough. A trifecta of tension has spurred badly labored breathing. The early start, the biting cold, and the sheer horror of it all have caused me to gulp in lung-blistering oceans of icy air. The problem is not too little oxygen, but too much. My chest hurts as if I've already covered forty miles.

"Calm down," I say softly. "Breathe normally. Quit straining. Quit gasping. Take it easy."

My whispers freak out a twentysomething in a neon green vest who eyes me suspiciously. He speeds up and pulls away. After several minutes, I feel the muscles around my ribs relaxing, then my back, then my shoulders, and then my neck. The pounding behind my eyes softens. My breathing becomes less ragged. Blood begins to warm the tissues of my lungs faster than the air can cool them. I know that I've already paid a price by taxing them so badly so early, but at least now I feel as if I am back in control and can limit the damage.

Second, there are my legs. When you run great distances, your legs have to be seen as both an interlocking system of joints, ligaments, tendons, and muscles—any one of which can betray you faster than a congressman—and simultaneously as a complete entity that can suffer a system-wide red alert for no apparent reason. The parts, at this point, seem good enough. My feet are comfortable, with no excessive sliding or hints of blisters. My knees feel the pressure of all the hills and all the weeks of heavy mileage but are otherwise solid. My calves, thighs, and butt muscles are tight but not cramping. My hips are pain-free.

Taken as a whole, however, my legs are shakier than expected. A nervous buzz is shooting through them. In a shorter race, the jitters wouldn't matter. Here they represent a useless waste of energy I can't afford, like a rocket spewing fuel through a leaky valve into the cosmic vacuum. Just as I did with my lung issue, I start talking my way through the problem.

"Relax. Not too much effort. Smooth strides. Muscles nice and soft. Loosen up. Come on."

The buzz fades. Once again, I know my inability to control my nerves earlier may prove disastrous later on. For the moment, however, my legs are settled. My strides feel, if not strong, at least not weak.

And with the pack to guide me, I am not lost. So there's that.

TWENTY-TWO

I have a half-dozen other things to keep an eye on: whether my clothing is rubbing, whether my stomach is upset, how tight my shoelaces are, and so on. On a normal run, none of them would be a serious threat. But just as an ultramarathon magnifies traditional mileage, it also magnifies problems. A waistband that irritates you during an hour-long workout can feel as if it is sawing you in half in a twelve-hour run. A water bottle that bumps your hip for six miles can pound up a bruise in forty-six. A race bib that flaps back and forth enough to annoy you in five miles can have you gnawing the bark from trees after fifty.

I'm relying on equipment that I've tested. I have a long-sleeve white PolyPro top, a gray Georgia Tech T-shirt, and a blue top over both for warmth. I have a thin stocking cap, lightweight cotton gloves, and my favorite running shoes. I also have my Bat Belt stuffed with Gatorade, sport beans, and my cell phone to keep Linda apprised of my progress. The best I can figure, no serious issues are arising with anything. My shorts fit. My water bottles are behaving. My number is secure.

There is, however, still the most important system on the checklist. Nothing can make you drop out sooner than letting your head run wild with a little nagging voice in the back of your brain saying one simple word: *Quit*. In a short race, it's easy to ignore; the effort and suffering are going to last only a few minutes or an hour. Even in a half marathon, the voice can be shouted down. But in a race that will last from sunrise to sunset and cover dozens of miles, that voice has a long time to work. *Quit. Quit. Quit.* No matter how much confidence you have at the start, no matter how much training you've put in, it can beat on your brain, wearing you down. This is, beyond the physical challenges, truly unknown territory for a first-time ultrarunner.

I keep hearing a conversation that I had with Linda a few days ago.

"I have a question," she said on the way home from my nerve-rattling test run on that nine-mile section of trail. "What is the greatest length of time you've run preparing for this race?"

We'd been in the car for twenty minutes, and I'd downed a Diet Coke, so I was feeling better. "About five hours."

"How many times have you done that?"

"Probably eight times in the past month."

"What else?"

"Well, nothing longer than that."

She arched an eyebrow. "So you've never run six straight hours in your life?"

"Uh, no."

"Never? Not even once?"

"No."

"But you're going to run over twice that long all in one day, up hills, through creeks, dodging trees, and in the cold?"

"Um . . ."

"And part of the time it will be dark?"

I'd never considered this race in those terms. I knew I was taking on a lot, in the same way that I know there are a lot of people in China. It was an abstraction. Fully grasping the reality was a different matter. I was going to spend an entire day running, dealing with that little voice saying, *Quit*.

The conversation with Linda is still in my mind as cold, gray light filters into the woods. One by one, we click off our headlamps, and when we reach an aid station, we drop them with the race volunteers. "We'll have them ready for you when you come back by," they say, as if delighted that we'll still be running when the sun goes back down. "See you later!" they say.

Much later, I think. We run a hundred yards down one of the rare stretches of paved road, climb over a traffic railing, and drop to the side of a creek, where the Greenway Trail picks up again.

The course continues swooping up and down hills—some bigger, some smaller, all to be reckoned with. I roll along as the sun slants through the leaves, and I'm feeling reasonably good when we hit the first creek crossing. The trail map suggests that we'll have to ford a dozen of these before the day is done. Deep or shallow is unclear. I'm already discovering that ultrarunners don't trouble themselves too much with such details. I recall photos from past Stone Mill races showing one particularly large crossing with runners clinging to a safety rope while sloshing through a rushing, knee-deep stream, and I wonder when we'll reach it. However, this first creek is small, and after I scramble around a couple of boulders, I leap across easily.

"One down, feet still dry," I mumble as I lean forward and dig up the opposite bank. I want to keep my shoes from getting wet for as long as possible, want to protect my feet from uncomfortable cold and potentially debilitating blisters. I'm disappointed when, on the very next crossing, I once again prepare for a big leap, only to feel my right foot slip sideways off a rock and shoot into the muck. The icy shock runs up my leg, sending a shiver through my frame.

"So much for that plan," I say to no one. I add it to the list of strategies that I am adjusting.

For example, I'm not walking all the uphills the way the ultra guides instructed, but I'm not precisely running them either. Like a lot of the others, I drop into a bent-knee shuffle each time a big slope comes our way, as if I am trying to sneak to the top undetected. Up where the course is flatter, I cruise at a comfortable pace. For the descents, I let my legs flow loosely. My plan seems to be working so far.

The pack is relatively intact. The rabbits are gone, of course, and presumably a few souls are straggling far behind, but the rest of us have spread out nicely to form a broad center of competitors. People are smiling and talking. We pass under a high, arched bridge that looks vaguely Gothic, and as if on cue, a giant Frankenstein of a man heaves into view. He runs with a peculiar gait, moving his legs primarily from the knees down. He has a barrel chest and is wearing spiderweb-patterned gaiters around his ankles to keep stones out of his shoes. Feeling a half-dozen pebbles shifting around my toes, I make a mental note to look into a pair if I survive.

"Hi, I'm Frank," he says. (Actually, I can't remember his name, but his size and the moment we met beneath that bridge made him eternally Frank in my mind.) "How's it going?"

"Good," I tell him. "Nice day for running."

"Hell yeah, it is. That's what I told my wife every morning for ten years. Now she's my ex-wife."

I laugh out loud. He doesn't crack a smile, so I can't tell if he intended to be funny. I try to get back on track, since I don't want an awkward relationship running alongside me all day. "Is this your first ultra?"

"No," he says. "I've run a bunch of them."

That seems unlikely. His style is so jerky and top-heavy— the way I'd look if I were smuggling a kindergartner in a backpack. I take him at his word. "This is my first. So is this one kind of average, or kind of hard, or kind of easy, or what?"

"I'm going to go with 'what.'"

This time he smiles.

"Just kidding," he says. "The thing is, you never really know how a race like this is going to be until you're in it. Even when you run a course that you've been on before, it can throw changes at you. Mud, or high water, or rain, or maybe you just eat the wrong thing for breakfast. Any of that can make an ultra harder or easier. Don't get me wrong. There are some sons-of-bitching courses out there that will break you ten times before you are halfway done. But most of the time it's not the course that decides if the race is rough. It's you. By the way, do you have a pacer?"

"What do you mean?"

"Don't you have somebody out here running with you?"

"No. Why?"

"Oh man," Frank says, and rolls his eyes. "It's just a lot easier if you have someone alongside who has done one of these before, who understands when it is going to get hard, and how to talk you through it, and how to keep you from giving up. Without that . . ." His voice fades, as if he's imagining my broken body in a dark ravine long after sunset, number flapping softly in an unexpected snowfall, sightless eyes staring. I'm wondering if I might ask him to stick with me for the day when he snaps out of his reverie.

"Anyway, I got to pee," he says and vaults into the trees. "See you later."

At that moment, I have two competing thoughts. One, I'll never see him again, because he runs in such a strange way that he can't be fast enough to ever catch me. And two, I could be terribly wrong. About him. About myself. About the whole idea that running fifty miles is something that normal humans can do. After all, even Frankenstein has just gone into the woods searching for relief.

TWENTY-THREE

One of the peculiarities of ultrarunning is the mood swings. When you're out in the woods for such a long time contemplating mortality, emotional ups and downs come along as often as the hills. Big ones. Frances Farmer changes in attitude. When I met Frank, I was feeling positive. When I left him, I was feeling irritable, pensive, and slightly scared again. Mysteriously, twenty minutes later I am again on the rebound.

I have left the woods for the only stretch of the race that resembles civilization on a large scale. For one glorious mile, I will run on a concrete sidewalk with cars zooming by. I'll whiz past coffee shops, a McDonald's, a school, a shopping center, and a housing subdivision. Some of the other runners disdain this part of the course, as if they're going to be forced to grab pizza at a Chuck E. Cheese. Not me. I'm all for a day in the woods, but this brief visit to planet Earth is heavenly. Even more so is the sight of Linda standing by the road, urging me on with a hot sausage biscuit, a cold Diet Coke, and a doughnut.

"I didn't know what you'd want, so I brought everything," she yells. "You look great!"

I should. I've covered only ten miles. Nothing at all, really. However, considering how I looked at this same point one week ago, I can appreciate her surprise.

"I feel good," I say.

"Any falls?"

"Not yet. I got my feet wet."

"They'll dry."

She trots alongside as I scarf bits of biscuit and hunks of doughnut and drain the soda. I probably don't need so much right now, but it is comfort food. As it settles into my stomach, I am optimistic.

"How are the legs?" she asks.

"Pretty springy. Let's see how they are when I get to the mill."

"I'm going home to wake up Ali, and we'll try to catch you down on the canal."

The idea that the rest of the world is barely stirring is intriguing. As I give her a quick kiss and take to the woods again, where the trail winds behind some houses. I wonder what it is like for the folks who are just waking up to look over their Pop-Tarts and see an army of lunatics lumbering through the countryside. Chances are that they may see a good bit more. Races like these tax the body so hard that nature doesn't just call; she shouts, *"Hey, you! Get over here!"*

I have been running away from my wife (so to speak) for only fifteen minutes when I'm reminded of how that can occur. I'm cruising in the vicinity of a young woman in a neon-green running top. She is small and quick, a compact runner who looks highly efficient. Accordingly, she boosts my confidence. Trail logic works this way: She is running strong. I am running near her. Ergo, I am running strong. For no good reason, I think of her as Susie. Susie Strong.

For several miles we have been trading places by a few dozen yards. At times I've surged ahead, thinking Susie has slowed and I may as well leave her. Then, minutes later, she'll slip past me, and I'll be the one playing catch-up. Although we've exchanged no more than a polite "Go ahead," when we pass in a tight spot, it is a good distraction. Every middle-of-the-packer knows the importance of these races within the race. They can keep you engaged for miles when the drudgery of the task is trying to pound all hope out of you. You pick a target and set your sights on outdistancing him or her, and for a time you can forget the bigger picture. You tell yourself, *"I won't win the race, I won't even place in my division, but by golly I'm going to beat this person."*

That's on my mind when Susie and I burn into one of the race checkpoints and aid stations. I shout out my number to an older woman sitting in a folding chair, keeping track of everyone with a clipboard. She calls back, "Thanks!" Another volunteer tops off my bottles with fresh sports drink, and I make a mistake. I grab a cookie. In that instant, a streak of neon green shoots into the trees, and Susie is gone. Somehow she'd negotiated the pit stop more efficiently, and by the time I can dust off the Toll House morsels and kick off in pursuit, she is out of sight on the winding path.

The temptation to sprint is strong. I want to rip up behind her, feet pounding, chest thrusting out, and my laughter thundering through the woods as I scorch past. Fortunately, I know better than to launch such a desperate counterattack. I tell myself there is plenty of time to catch her. What I did not know, but will learn throughout the day, is an interesting quirk of distance running and gender. Pound for pound, step for step, women are considerably better ultrarunners than are men. Researchers have tried to pin down all the reasons and have developed several theories. The first has something to do with estrogen. Without getting into all the chemistry, gals can process fat cells more readily than guys can. So while we men are furiously throwing our carbs into the fire of our effort, women are running on a more efficient mix of carbs and fats. It's as if they have a natural fuel additive that increases their gas mileage.

The second most common theory is that childbirth has, in an evolutionary sense, made women better at withstanding pain. So in the late stages of the race, when everyone is hurting, they can endure it better.

My own addition to this field of study is a tad more direct. I think guys are kind of stupid. Many of us never quite let go of the teenage bravado that spurred us to jump off rooftops into swimming pools, skateboard surf behind cars, and attempt all manner of stunts that formed the backbone of the *Jackass* television series. Accordingly, guys are more likely to persuade themselves to start extreme runs with inadequate training, nagging injuries, or any number of other things that would make a more reasonable person reconsider. Many women, on the other hand, are more honest about their abilities. They, too, may be out to prove something, because they are as competitive as anyone else, but they are smarter about their preparation.

All of that means the fastest men will still win most of the big events, but the longer the race goes, the more women close the gap, and those in the middle of the pack will give the men all they can handle. In short, fewer women than men show up for these events, but those women who do ought to be feared.

I am blissfully unaware of all this as I cruise through the woods around mile 15, waiting to reel Susie back in. My legs are fully warm, the fuel from my fast breakfast has replenished my system, and I feel strong. Maybe the idea that Frankenstein is lumbering after me somewhere back there is helping, but for whatever reason, I am luxuriating in the movement. The houses have long since disappeared. The hills have resumed. Every so often I come to another creek, most of which I jump successfully, some of which I don't. The trail remains buried in leaves, and the threat of tripping remains ever present. None of it matters. My feet glide effortlessly, and I have been upping my pace for several miles, passing other runners who are moving slowly. I'm even charging up some of the hills as if they are flatlands. Then I catch a flash of neon green in the trees ahead: Susie.

One of my favorite racing techniques from youth was to slip in behind a challenger and ride his heels, assessing his condition and the likelihood that he'd fight back, before I rocketed past. I move up within twenty feet of Susie, softening my footfalls so that I make almost no noise. In the hush of the woods, I can hear her raspy breathing. Occasionally she sucks in a sharp breath, as if she's in pain. Her stride is slightly uneven, and she is buckling forward somewhat. I suspect that she has been trying to open an insurmountable gap between us and is now paying for that hubris. I'm loading up to pass when she cuts hard off the trail, staggers into the brush, and yanks at her shorts as she disappears behind a big tree.

In an instant I realize what's wrong. She has miscalculated her eating and drinking. Her system is in revolt, her gastro-intestinal tract has summoned Susie to a reckoning. It's not fatal. It's not even that serious in terms of overall health, but it is a hazard that can lay waste to the best race plan. As I speed by, my sense of victory evaporates along with much of the confidence on which I've been feeding. I didn't catch her because I was so fast, but because she was operating at half strength.

Minutes ago I was intent on mowing her down. Now I find myself hoping she can pull it together and get back on course. I'm learning another lesson of ultras: No other runner is your enemy. The course is. We all have to encourage and watch out for one another because we're engaged in an activity that could go very wrong at any moment for any one of us. And only a few minutes after I watch Susie trip off into the woods, I discover a fresh problem of my own. The enthusiasm of the past few miles has pushed me into one of the most basic, insidious, and potentially race-ending mistakes any runner can make, especially in an ultra.

As I pass the next checkpoint, I call out to a volunteer, "Where am I?"

She's wearing a warm jacket, gloves, and an encouraging smile. "Twenty miles," she shouts back, as if telling me I've won the lottery.

I look at my watch and hiss, "Son of a bitch."

I am running way, way, way too fast. I warned myself against this. I trained to prevent it. I pulled back hard on my mental throttle, starting with the first step, and yet I've allowed it to happen. In a race of this length, I am effectively exploding on the launch pad.

It's not like I am poised to vault into the lead or anything like that. The frontrunners are already pushing hard toward the final quarter of the race, and there is no chance that I'm going to magically pass them, seize the first-place trophy, and shock the ultra community with a post-race interview in *Runner's World*.

"Tom, you started ultrarunning only a few months ago, you're over fifty, and somehow you came out here and decimated an entire field of great competitors with a new course record. How did you do it?"

"Beats the shit out of me, Chuck."

That's not going to happen. Unfortunately, a reasonable alternative isn't going to happen either. This early blast of hill-eating energy isn't going to lead me to some magnificent time in my first 50-miler. To the contrary, I am deeply disturbed because I know what is taking place.

Another man who would have known, had he been with me, was Jöns Jacob Berzelius. Way back in 1808, when the whole concept of people running for fun was highly suspect and the notion of running an ultramarathon would have been cause for confinement, Berzelius was a Swedish chemist with groundbreaking ideas about molecules, electricity, and chemical reactions. He pioneered work in atomic theory, is largely credited with the creation of chemical notation, and was no doubt always given a great table at whatever restaurant the Swedish chemistry crowd frequented.

One day, he extracted some liquid from a piece of stag meat. Why, I don't know—I've always assumed he lost some kind of bet. Anyway, he discovered something hiding in that fluid that no one had noticed before: lactic acid. The acid had been previously noted in a cup of sour milk by another scientist (hence the "lactic") but never before in a hunk of steak. Berzelius wondered what this stuff was doing in his entrée, and he came up with a theory the way geniuses do. He thought the lactic acid might be there because the stag had been running when it was killed, and in that moment he became the first researcher to draw a link between exercise and the buildup of this fluid. Over the next half century, other researchers established a clear cause and effect. When we exercise, lactic acid appears. If we have enough oxygen flowing to our muscles, it will carry the acid away and all will be well. But if we exert ourselves so long or hard that the oxygen cannot keep up with the lactic acid, our muscles will drown in it. They grow tired, sore, and eventually refuse to function, no matter how much a person may want to push on. Let motivational speakers say what they will, chemistry trumps psychology. Where there is a will, there is not necessarily a way.

Fearing that Berzelius's discovery is already taking a horrible toll on me, I slam on the brakes to walk and reassess. I can't feel the effects yet, but I know that my watch is not lying and that at this pace I'm going to enter what ultrarunners call the "pain cave" a lot earlier than expected. There are only two ways to mitigate the damage, neither particularly effective. I can get a lot more careful about what I am eating. If I make sure that every bite is as fuel-efficient as possible, I might be able to offset the pain with raw energy. Kind of like stepping on the gas harder because you realize your parking brake is stuck. The problem is, I've never more than skimmed those articles with titles like "Ten Best Foods for Running" and "Fast Foods for Fast Races!" It has always seemed to me that the folks writing such things were taking this sport far too seriously. As a result, I have no idea whether a peanut butter sandwich, a brownie, or a dill pickle will serve me best.

I can also ease up on my pace, but that's not a choice. My body is going to force me to slow down in short order anyway. Even then I will still be moving. The lactic acid will be pooling in my muscles more slowly, but pooling nonetheless. And the slower I run, the more time I will spend out here. It's a devil's decision with potential calamity on either side. Run faster and hurt more, or run slower and hurt longer.

These are crappy choices, and I am wrestling with them as I hit a series of hills where the path has been heavily used by horseback riders and is filled with ruts. The trail bucks and heaves, pounding my frame. Muddy hoofprints grab at my soles. My ankles snap, crackle, and pop. I dip and dodge to avoid smacking my head into hardwood or poking an eye out with a twig.

When I finally hit a short stretch of meadow, I am feeling the first wave of serious fatigue. I still don't know what I can or should do in response, but deep inside my legs I know the clock is ticking.

TWENTY-FOUR

R un, Dad, run!"

Ali wears a huge grin as I steam up the canal path around mile 22, and I force a smile in return. She is waving a hand-lettered sign with the same words, and she dashes over to jog with me. Seeing her and Linda raises my spirits, which could use the help. For the past few miles I've enjoyed running by the river on this short section of the towpath, but only in a relative sense. It is less challenging than the hills, but I am grinding badly and my outlook is dismal.

"How are you doing?" Linda asks the perpetual question as I run to give her a hug.

"Okay," I say. "Feeling it a bit."

Ali says, "We tried to catch you at the last aid station, but they told us you'd already passed."

"You're way ahead of schedule, aren't you?" Linda says, heedless of what that means. The Stone Mill is just ahead. It is the turning point, where we stop heading out and start heading back to where we began.

"Yeah, I guess that's the good news, huh?" I reply.

"Doing all right on your liquids?" she asks.

"Well enough." I'm disguising my concerns to relieve her doubts, and she seems to buy it. She pats me on the shoulder.

"Grab a picture, Mom," Ali says, posing with me where the path crosses a small bridge. After the camera clicks, Ali hugs me and says, "Better get going, you running animal!"

I laugh and move off, lifting my feet enough to suggest boundless energy. As soon as I am out of their sight, I slip back into a shuffle. I've stabilized my speed, and I've settled on a more realistic pace, but energy is seeping out of my pores in a slow, deadly leak. The idea of turning back into the hills is mortifying. They have already pounded me much more than I thought possible, and I am feeling pain in wholly new places. That said, my desperation has spawned a plan for survival.

The Stone Mill is a massive, beautiful old ruin of cut rock tumbling down in the woods. Red sandstone walls loom as a crumbling castle over a tangle of weeds and briars. Massive windows and doors, long ago stripped of their wooden frames, give a sense of gigantic scale, and channels through the earth show where great waterwheels turned the machinery back when it was bustling with men cutting stone blocks to build the canal, the lock houses, and a tavern or two. It is really quite lovely in a fading way.

And I miss it entirely.

Even though it is just yards from the left side of the race-course and easily visible, I am fixated on the aid station to the right. Some aid stations are small, but this one is huge. Runners are sprawled in the grass, changing socks, smearing Vaseline over friction spots, and slapping tape on bleeding toes. I run up to the food table and begin plundering its grilled cheese, candy, chips, and Mountain Dew. I've decided that I must dramatically increase my intake. I'm convinced that I haven't been eating or drinking nearly enough to sustain myself, and this, in addition to my excessive speed, is the reason I'm crashing. From here on out, I will keep my pace under control and force-feed myself like a pet lizard.

Just having this idea is helpful, compared with the hopeless fog I've been running through. I grab brownies, pretzels, and Fig Newtons and jam them into my mouth. A fistful of M&M's is followed by a peanut butter sandwich and a stack of chocolate chip cookies. All of it tastes great. I briefly entertain the notion of abandoning the race right here, standing by the table, and stuffing my face until they chase me off or call an ambulance.

In a couple of minutes I feel restored enough to release that idea, and I pull out of the aid station with renewed commitment. I notice a young guy in a tan T-shirt who is running well, and I fall in with him.

"You're looking fresh," I say. "You must have run a few of these before."

"This is my first," he replies. "I've been in some marathons, but nothing like this. Actually, I'm not sure I've trained enough."

He looks rock solid and is moving like a Maserati, despite some odd bootlike running shoes, so either he's being falsely modest or I'm in more trouble than I think.

"What sort of schedule have you been following?" I ask.

"I'm in the Air Force, so I work out pretty much every day before my duty, but I haven't always been able to do as many miles as I would like."

"My dad was in the Air Force. My brother too. My name is Tom."

"I'm Larry."

"Where are you from?"

"Originally from New Mexico, but now I'm based out here. What do you do for a living?"

"I'm a journalist. Work for CNN. What about you?"

I sense tension, and Larry gets vague. "I do special work."

"Like what?"

"Just special projects for the Air Force."

"Yeah. Like what?"

"Tell me about your training," he says. "You're looking good."

His retreat from telling any details about himself is something I've seen before with military folks, most often with those who are involved in Special Forces. I drop a step and look him over again. Chiseled frame, steady movement, and quick, searching eyes. I'm guessing Air Force Special Operations Command. He won't tell me, of course, but that doesn't matter. I already know what I need to know: He will be an excellent guy to draft off for a while.

Tagging onto the back of stronger competitors, if they're not burning up the course, is a sure way to make your run easier. You slip in behind them, forget any worries about pacing, and hang on. When they go faster, slow down, or take a drink, you do too. It's a mindless way of running, but sometimes it's just the ticket during a tough slog, and I've been struggling with both my body and brain for so long today that I can use the break.

Apparently, others can as well. In the mile of flat dirt road after the aid station, a tiny knot of runners has coalesced. No one has planned it, but, as in the old C. W. McCall song, we find ourselves in a convoy—or as ultrarunners call it, "a bus." Ten runners have fallen in behind Larry and me, and as if they can sense his discipline and natural leadership, they form a tight trailing line as we turn back into the woods. The leaves swish to life beneath our feet, and the hills begin kicking up and down with the same sadistic rhythm that has been torturing us all day.

The bus doesn't care. Buoyed by the combined energy of the group, each one of us surges with strength. Lighthearted conversations break out. A guy in the back makes a joke I can't hear, and laughter ripples up the line. The sun is shining through the trees, and another person looks at the GPS unit in his phone. "Twenty-five miles!" he calls out. "More than halfway!" A cheer rises and we thunder on.

Without moments like these, I suspect many more runners wouldn't make it through. For such a lonely sport, it is odd how united runners can feel when circumstance and the relentless challenge of big miles put them in the same place at the same time. There is a profound sense of teamwork. We are in this together against the cold, against the darkness, against the hills, the leaves, the roots, the rocks, and the streams. Our group is heavy with young, strong runners—guys who, like Larry, appear to be entirely at ease, as if they'd hopped onto the trail a few miles ago and expect to be done in thirty minutes. There is also an older woman named Sonya who is moving with steady grace. She and I chat about how nice the weather is, all things considered, because it's not raining.

After a while, the bus quiets down, just like on a real vehicle on a cross-country trip, with everyone slipping into his or her thoughts. The talking stops. Nothing but the swish of our feet and our breathing fills the woods.

The hills are medium size and fairly steep, so we are constantly climbing or descending and everyone is focused. Now and then we hit a flat section, and at one point we cross a road. A family of four is camped in lawn chairs by their car with signs to wave for some runner somewhere in the pack. We nod hello and glide past, and then the forest swallows us again. I've avoided looking at my watch for some time, and I've lost any sense of how far we've traveled. It seems as if it has been a while.

"Do you know what our mileage is?" I ask Sonya, who is just behind me.

"I think we must be getting close to thirty."

"Sounds about right."

I pull out my phone. Despite the deepness of the woods and the ravines, I am able to text my position to Linda: *30 miles . . . I think*. I slip the phone back into my pack and take a quick drink of Gatorade, and the bus turns up another steep, short hill.

How the next transition comes upon me, I can't really say. I am feeling better about where I am in the race, encouraged about my new fueling plan, and optimistic that this day is going to turn out okay after all. I round a corner at the top, and on the descent calamity strikes.

My toes have been pinging off hard things beneath the leaves with alarming frequency, and now my right foot snags on a small chunk of granite that won't let go. I snap my left foot up late as my weight shifts, and that toe catches too. I pitch forward. My knees rip into the trail, and my hands shoot out. I bounce back to my feet, losing little more than a stride, amid a chorus of calls from the bus. "Are you okay? Are you hurt?"

"I'm fine," I say. "Sorry for holding us up."

I reestablish my position in the line with a painful blast of adrenaline in my veins. My knees are more dirty than damaged. My good humor is replaced by an angry voice in my head cursing my clumsiness, warning me to stay alert, to pick my feet up, and to watch for trouble. Then, impossibly, it happens again.

We've traveled less than a quarter mile from my first fall, and again my right toe finds a stone. Again, I can't react quickly enough, and my weight rushes forward across my center of balance. My hands reach out, only this time with a sickening difference. As my knees strike, my right hand jams with savage force against a root beneath the leaves. I hear a crack. Pain fires through my wrist, the shock jolting up my arm. I curse, twist, and fall to the side of the path.

"Are you all right?" a chorus of voices calls out again, this time with deeper concern, the worried sound of runners who think they may have a problem on their hands.

"Yeah," I grumble. "I'm fine. Go on ahead. I need to regroup."

The bus takes my word and rumbles away as I rise again and start jogging very slowly after them, breathing and moving heavily. My knees are burning with dirt mixed into the bloody scrapes. The toe that caught both the first and second rocks feels as if someone has stomped on it, but the real problem is my hand. That snap I heard was either the tree root or one of my bones, and the heel of my right thumb says it was the latter. It is throbbing. I gently push and pull at it, feeling for any grinding or cracking, and then I roll the hand over and see a dark bloodstain spreading through my glove. I peel the thin cotton back enough to look, dreading that I will find a sliver of bone slicing through the meat. There is only a small gash, but the area around it is purple and swelling fast. The skin is tightening, and the fever of injury is engulfing my forearm. Each beat of my pulse is a hammer strike on the ball of my thumb.

I pull the glove back into place over the wound and curse my clumsiness and fatigue. "Stupid, stupid, stupid."

I look around, trying to calculate how I will get out of here if my thumb is broken and if the swelling and pain intensify to the point that I can't run. There is no easy exit. To be honest, I have no idea where I am. My hand throbs. My legs ache. Up ahead I catch one last glimpse of the bus roaring over a distant hill.

I trudge on, alone.

TWENTY-FIVE

The sun, flickering behind bare branches, has passed its zenith. The temperature has barely cracked 50 degrees and is already retreating. It's a blessing. I'm another hour farther down the trail, and the growing cold has stopped the swelling in my hand. The bleeding has stopped as well, and the pain has subsided. I've ceased wondering if I will catch the bus again. It is long gone.

"How's it going?"

The booming voice startles me. It's Frank, lurching along just as he was when I met him a lifetime ago. I'm dismayed that he has caught me, yet happy to see a familiar face.

"Other than a broken thumb, I'm doing fine."

"Dude! Seriously?"

"Not seriously. I thought it was for a while, but now I think I just jammed it. I fell."

"You and everyone else."

I have noticed that a lot of my compatriots have also taken tumbles. Some have dirty knees, scraped shins, or bruised elbows. Some are caked with mud in odd places. A few even look as if they've T-boned trees with their foreheads.

"Have you fallen?" I ask Frank.

"Not yet, knock wood. I probably will before I'm done, but maybe not. I'm taking it easy today."

Not exactly what I want to hear. Just minutes ago I had pulled out my phone to text Linda that I was still trundling on.

Woo hoo, she'd typed back. *Go, Tom, go!*

She might have been less enthusiastic if she'd realized how much I was feeling the miles. My calves are as tight as ticks on a cow's ass. So if Frank considers this "taking it easy" I may yet be in big trouble. And then there is the matter of Cat.

Some miles back the trail entered a series of farm fields. There was a small apple orchard, a broad meadow, and a couple of kids perched on a hay wagon like a scene from a 1940s documentary made by the Agriculture Department. The ground rolled gently. The small trees were spaced wider with tall grasses dominating the ground instead of leaves. It was pleasant, in the same sense that even in prison some cells are better than others, and part of what made this stretch enjoyable was a little drama I was watching around a young woman in a pink hoodie and black capri running pants.

She appeared to be in her late twenties, with long blond hair and a pleasant face. She was running with a red-bearded guy about her age who was lightly built and looked like he was serving as a pacer. For several miles we were in one another's orbits. I would pass them and disappear up the trail, and then they'd catch me, pass, and do their own vanishing act. Each time, I'd hear him encouraging her and giving gentle advice about the terrain and her pacing, liquids, and stride. For no good reason, I thought of him as Rick. He called her Cat.

Cat did not look like a runner. Her stride was flat-footed

and short. She wasn't large, but she wasn't tiny. Her shoulders and arms looked less like the swift bird wings of an Olympic runner and more like the sleek, powerful tools of a swimmer. Her back was plastered with sweat. Each time we exchanged places, I could hear her panting and see her concentration. I didn't think she was long for this race.

So I had been tracking her progress, watching each time she stumbled or walked a few steps, trying to gauge how much she was laboring to gulp oxygen. I was steps behind her and Rick when we turned a corner near the end of the fields and faced a wide, muddy bog near a pasture. It was hemmed hard by briars, and so many runners had already passed through that it was awash with black, soupy muck, which wafted the piquant aroma of rotting weeds and animal dung.

"Oh no!" These were the first words I'd heard from Cat, and they were laced with dismay. There was only a dim hope of keeping our feet dry, and that rested entirely on our ability to balance like a Wallenda. A rickety lattice of half-submerged, broken branches stretched from the dry bank where we stood to the far shore thirty feet away. If every step was chosen and executed perfectly (not an easy trick when your legs feel as if they have been crushed beneath a Buick), there was a slim chance of escaping the bog. If not, one's shoes would get wet. Really wet. Deep, dirty, sloppy, smelly, "you're not bringing those shoes into this house, in fact just throw them away" wet.

Rick went first. His initial efforts were promising. He moved out over the mire cautiously, toes testing the branches, hovering above the shimmering goo. He was a few steps from safety when he splashed in, squishing down to his ankles. When he pulled free, his feet made such a sucking sound that

I wondered if he'd still have his socks as he climbed up on the opposite shore.

"Dammit," Cat said, watching him emerge.

"C'mon. We've got to get moving," he called back.

She looked over her shoulder at me as if I might have a pontoon bridge in my pocket. "Go ahead," I said helpfully.

She stepped as gingerly as she could onto the branches, teetering left, right, forward, and back all at once. Her hands flailed elaborately. Her feet moved with dreadful indecision. Little yips came with each waver. It was entertaining, but I was losing too much time waiting, so I stepped out and caught up to her about halfway across.

"Woooo hoooo!" A wild young guy emerged from somewhere behind us, skipping the balancing act on the branches altogether and stomping through the slough, spraying water and mud. It was too much for Cat. Her fragile equilibrium collapsed and she fell backward. I grabbed at her, she grabbed at me, and somehow we remained upright, but the violent movement drove our feet into the swamp. Mud and water oozed into my shoes, as icy and revolting as a cowshit shake. For form's sake, we both stepped back onto the branches and made a perfunctory effort to stay aloft until the opposite side, but the damage was done. Cat, Rick, and I all ran away with blackened feet and moods to match.

I figured that was it for Cat. The final straw. The hook. The song of the fat lady. I was tired and miserable, and I was running stronger than she was, so how could it be otherwise?

At the next aid station, I know I am right. Frank and I rumble in together, with Cat and company on our tail, but she is tortured. She staggers with barely enough strength to reach for an Oreo. I see Rick trying to talk her out of her half-collapsed, hands-on-knees stance. A few other friends are there to cheer her on. They keep patting her back, and her legs look as if they'll buckle under the touches. They are saying things that are alternately encouraging and consoling. I hang around munching chips, waiting to see if she can get moving again. I finally give up, heading out with Frank as she slumps in defeat.

It's a shame, really.

Maybe the rabbit runners up front like to see a challenger fold, but no middle-packer does. We are the brotherhood and sisterhood of also-rans, and every time one of us abandons the race, it rekindles the fear and weakness in us all, making us look over our shoulders, wondering if fatigue, cramps, dehydration, nausea, and injury are coming for us too. As I grind past mile 37, I find myself missing Cat. Like dozens of others I've seen fall out of races over the past year, she deserves better. She has undoubtedly trained obscenely long hours for many months. She likely has blisters, sore calves, aching thighs, and all the other maladies we've all endured to be here today. She ran harder and farther than most people ever will in their lifetimes. She endured the bitter cold with all of us this morning, the darkness, the hills, the ankle-twisting ravines, and filthy, wet feet—everything that I have endured—and it isn't enough.

Apparently Frank's training isn't enough, either. By the time I reach the next aid station, he has nodded me on and quietly slipped far behind. I am once again running alone.

"Yay! All right, bring it on!" The volunteers cheer as if I am in the chase for the lead, even though the winners long ago crossed the finish line, and this aid station is seeing runners only every five or ten minutes now. The race rules have allowed each of us to prepare "drop bags"—nylon totes with clean shirts, Band-Aids, special snacks, whatever—and those bags are waiting for us here. All I want are fresh shoes and socks. I flop onto the grass to change, and the shock of sitting for the first time in more than eight hours is overwhelming. My back, my legs, my shoulders, my head, my stomach, my feet, and even my hair hurt. For a moment I fear I may be unable to stand. Fortunately, I am on a slight slope, so I roll into an upright position, lightning crackling through my legs.

A nagging thought that has been with me from the start comes to mind once more: the cutoff. Most races of any length have a limit on how long you can be out there running. After all, at some point, race volunteers have to go home, parking lots need to be cleared, Porta-Johns picked up, and roads reopened. Cutoffs are the tool to make all that happen. In shorter races they are based on the finish line. In longer runs, like marathons and ultras, runners must reach specific mile markers by specific times. Fail to make even one, and no matter how much you want to go on, you'll be pulled from the course.

The Stone Mill organizers said on the race website that they would be generous. If a runner missed a cutoff by a few minutes and looked strong, he or she would be allowed to press on. I don't want to test their patience.

"Am I doing all right on the cutoff?" I ask as I grab some chocolate chip cookies, gulp down a paper cup full of Mountain Dew, and started jogging away.

"You're fine," a volunteer yells. Then my heart jumps.

"No, wait!" another yells. "Come back!"

I turn around, ashen with fear.

"Your light. Don't forget it," he says, pointing to where all our headlamps from the morning have been laid out. I find mine, start breathing again, and run off into the hills.

How are you? Linda texts.

Okay. At about 40 miles I think, I respond.

I'm waiting for you at 41!

It is wonderful news. I feel a rush of sentiment, as if I want to cry. Even as slowly as I am running, I will be there in fifteen minutes, and then just nine miles will remain. Within seconds, however, something is horribly wrong. All day I have been able to force my way forward against every urge to stop. This is different. Almost as if I've been unplugged, my legs go dead. My feet strike the earth, and pulling them free is like fighting great magnets in the dirt. Worse, my will to do anything about it is gone.

I have entered the pain cave.

The pain cave sounds like something from one of those steamy bondage novels. There is nothing sexy about it. The pain cave is a mind-numbing place where all of one's reference points get lost. Normal pain, like you might feel from falling off a bicycle or from childbirth, arises from some dramatic event, intensifies, and then gradually recedes as its source is removed or grows up and goes to college. Fatigue is much the same. It comes. It goes. If it's really bad, you sleep in on Saturday morning.

In the pain cave, the hurt emanates from your core, radiating out and echoing back from everywhere and nowhere at once. Weird ripping sensations suggest your muscles are separating from your bones. Tendons feel as if they are shredding.

Your pulse thrums against the back of your skull and vibrates through your eye sockets. The fatigue is pervasive. My lungs sizzle with an exhaustion that creates an overwhelming desire to lie down on the trail and stop breathing.

If anyone asked me to confess any crime at that moment, I would have.

In physiological terms, all my systems are going haywire. My salts, sugars, and liquids are completely out of whack. My heart and lungs are no longer efficiently delivering oxygen. My muscles, dripping with lactic acid, are so desperate for energy they are eating themselves. My skin has become hypersensitive. The breeze burns against it. My shirt feels heavy on my shoulders. A seam of my shorts is sawing at my crotch. I feel alternately as if I am burning with fever and then freezing.

Interestingly, one of the most obvious symptoms of extreme exhaustion is an inability to recognize it: confusion, disorientation, difficulty concentrating. In more prosaic terms, my body is telling me that it has had enough of this shit, even if I'm too stupid to realize it.

I have read accounts of climbers on Mount Everest, up where the sun blisters the skin while the snow ices the blood, slipping into the pain cave so deeply that they sit down and wind up frozen in that spot forever. The only thing that can save someone in such a fix is the discipline born of training. You must have the unstoppable urge to put one foot ahead of the other even when there seems to be no reason to do so.

The best ultrarunners have it. The Hardrock 100 is a soul-crushing run through the Colorado Rockies that starts in the old mining town of Silverton at an elevation just over 9,000 feet and has more than a dozen climbs over 12,000. At the highest point, the runners cross Handies Peak at a lung-destroying 14,058 feet—more than two and a half miles in the air. Chipping away at the hundred-mile course in those conditions takes the kind of endurance that even most ultrarunners can scarcely imagine. The race has a forty-eight-hour limit, so even runners who can survive the agonizing climbs and descents (much of the time in the dark) must continually calculate their odds of finishing before the cutoff. More important, at that altitude, all the competitors are spending significant amounts of time on towering peaks where lightning furiously flashes across bare rock faces.

It is little wonder, then, that Adam Campbell was watching the skies as he tore along in the race in 2014. Campbell, who is an exceptionally talented endurance athlete from Canada in his mid-thirties, was running close by his pacer, Aaron Heidt, as they headed toward a peak being lit up by an electrical storm. As Campbell told Competitor.com, "There's nothing up there. No place to hide, no rocks, no trees, no nothing." So the two tried to dash over the top, and a moment later the ground shook. A blast of lightning leveled both of them. But that's not the amazing part. After they were nearly blown out of their shoes, the men stood up, decided they were unhurt, and finished the remaining forty miles of the race. Campbell came in third.

That is the resolve of a true ultrarunner.

It is also the last and most critical thing to leave you in the pain cave, and I feel it bleeding out of me onto the trail. My brain is sluggish and confused. In shorter runs, physical training is everything. In an ultra, mental toughness is just as critical. These races are too long for raw confidence. Here, you must stare failure in the face over and over without blinking, enduring the emptiness of these latter miles where there is no one to cheer, wave signs, or even say "Keep going," as a chorus in your head screams *Quit!* It is surreal. This is the kind of exercise Salvador Dalí and the Marquis de Sade would have come up with.

I have to justify every step against a twisted version of reality that defies analysis. I look at my watch and can't make sense of the pace. I look at my feet and realize I am walking. For how long, I don't know. I recall walking up a hill a while back, but when was that? Two minutes ago? Ten minutes? I wonder if I just forgot to start running again after walking around some obstacle or if I never intended to. The woods, the hills, and the terrain all blend into an unchanging brown collage in which nothing appears to be moving, least of all me.

I look behind. Not a soul. Ahead. No one. I can't imagine how everyone passed me without notice, and yet clearly that has happened. I am either lost or the last person out here, and the depression that comes with that realization is crushing.

I slap my hands hard against my thighs in anger. I barely feel it. I bend my knees and force out a dozen agonizing steps of running, growling between clenched teeth, "You've trained too hard to quit. You'll never forgive yourself if you give up. You'll hate this day forever." I look at my watch and up the trail. I should have reached Linda at the next aid station by now. "Where is she?"

And then, in the aching loneliness, I say something else.

"You'll never make it."

Just like that, the tank is dry. I slump into a walk again for half a dozen steps. Then I stop. I've run all those miles, suffered all that pain, asked my family and friends and coworkers to give me so much time to train, and now it is down to this inglorious end.

The cold, staved off by exertion all day, invades my body. I shiver and wonder how I will find a road, get help, and go home. I don't know how far it is to the next aid station or how long it will take me to walk there. I don't care. I don't know what has happened to Frankenstein, Susie, Rick, or Cat. I don't know what I will say to Linda or to Ali. I have no idea how I can explain this to Ronnie after all we went through and all my sermons about not giving up. I don't even know how I'll explain it to myself tomorrow.

All I know is that I have given an entire year of my life in slavish devotion to running: racking up workouts, ignoring other duties, pummeling my body through too many miles to remember. And now I am standing in the woods, too tired and hurt to take another step.

My race is over.

TWENTY-SIX

One of the less appreciated aspects of defeat is the freedom it brings. All expectations vanish. All notions of your goals float away. Gone is the tyranny of "what ought to be," and in its place arises the kinder, gentler cousin of "what might happen." Each moment of continued survival, which was a measure of defeat minutes ago, is now a tiny victory. The psychological boost of thinking this way can be remarkably uplifting.

It also helps to get a phone call.

"Hey, how's it going?" My brother's voice, cheerful and energetic, catches me off guard. I had started walking again because I had nothing better to do, and I needed to get out of the woods, but with each step I'd been surprised to find my mood improving. Contemplating the idea of sitting down and enjoying some hot chocolate and a warm shower was such a welcome change to the idea of droning on for two or three more hours that it was blunting the feeling of failure. And now this.

"Okay, I guess," I lie. "Actually, this is much tougher than I expected." I tell the truth. "My legs are just dead. I've been alone in the woods forever now. I haven't seen anyone except this eighty-year-old Korean guy who passed me ten minutes ago."

"There's an eighty-year-old Korean in the race?"

"No. I think he lives around here and he was out walking for exercise."

"And he passed you?" Robert laughs. "That's rough. So what are you going to do?"

"What do you suggest?"

"The only thing I've ever known to do: just focus on the next step, then the next one, then the next one, and keep doing that until you are at the finish line."

I look down at my plodding feet, which are miraculously still moving. "Sounds simple."

"It is. But for now, let's talk a little more."

And we do. We talk and laugh. He tells me about his trip home from the hospital and how his recovery is progressing. We share stories of our long-ago running days. The conversation takes only minutes but it feels like an hour. I forget about the race. The pain does not go away, but its sharp edge retreats. I could talk forever. Robert has other ideas.

"Look, this has been fun," he says, "but you need to get running again."

It isn't a question. I pause, then answer. "Okay. I'll give a shout when I'm done."

I shove the phone back into my belt and start running again. My legs feel just as bad. My body still howls for rest, but the break and pep talk have worked wonders. Moments later, the woods part and I find Linda waiting in the fading light by one of the last aid stations. She's been trading texts with friends.

"Judy was asking me if I saw buzzards," Linda tells me. "You look good." It is her turn to lie. My hair is disheveled. My face is gaunt. I look like Larry King emerging from the desert.

"Do you know how much farther I have to go?" I ask.

"About ten miles."

I look at my watch. "How did I slow down so much? I should have reached this point an hour ago."

"Yeah," she says, "around the finish line a lot of people are saying the course is running long. It's more than fifty miles."

"How many more?"

"I don't know, but it sounds like a lot. You better get going."

I'd heard a few rumbles from others with GPS. They'd been complaining that some of the mileage markers did not match reality. The race director had admitted a few days before the start that last-minute adjustments had lengthened the course by at least a mile, but this was shaping up as something more substantial.

Minutes after leaving Linda, on the last part of the race—a devilish out-and-back trek alongside a creek—I reluctantly switch on my headlamp and wonder how much darkness is ahead. Susie, Frank, Rick, and impossibly even Cat have all emerged from nowhere and passed me again. As I stagger along, I am grateful when a guy in his sixties named George and a thirtysomething named Charles hook up with me to form a minibus. It isn't much, but as the temperature drops and the evening deepens, they are good company. We talk about the day, the lights of other runners shining through the trees, and the startling fact that we are not the last people on the course. Indeed, it now appears that dozens of others are behind us.

The final portion is as hard as every earlier step. Harder. The trail is every bit as steep, narrow, and shrouded in leaves. The rocks snag my feet just as viciously, and we finally reach the great stream crossing I'd been looking for all day. It's a rushing tempest of bitterly cold water. I try to hold on to the guide rope stretched from one bank to another and to balance on rocks, until I realize that some of them, which appear to be above the water in my headlamp's beam, are actually a few inches below the surface. By the time I'm halfway across, my feet are so soaked that I step into the creek, sinking past my knees, and complete the crossing with no more regard for the cold. When I have to cross the stream again, I don't even hesitate. I jump off the embankment into the icy water and wade, clawing up the muddy bank on the far side. I am no longer even trying to avoid the pain and punishment but embracing them.

The final three miles are an eternity. The darkness is complete. The world exists only as a halo of light thrown by my headlamp on the ceaseless ground. George grabbed a slightly faster minibus as it passed, leaving Charles and me staggering together toward the line. He is from north of D.C. and ran several ultras earlier in the year.

"Too many," he tells me as we labor along. "I think I've just trashed my legs too much to do well today."

We talk about our families, our jobs, running, movies, books—anything to keep our minds off the fatigue and the descending night. That morning we'd both worn heavy tops to deal with the low temperatures. But we shed those long before noon, and we have nothing like that now. Every five minutes the cold gets worse.

"We have to keep moving," I joke, "or we'll freeze."

Then a wonderful thing happens. One instant we are pounding against the endless darkness and hateful trail, and the next we are in the final few hundred yards. The woods spread wide over a road crossing, close around us again, and then open for a final time to a steep grassy upslope. I drive my feet into the embankment and push myself upward for fifty yards toward the glowing red numbers of the race clock. The finish is brilliantly, blindingly flooded with light.

Just over 13 hours and 12 minutes after starting to run, I step across the line and stop.

There is no official measurement, but the best estimates put the course at 55 miles.

I am handed a medal. Linda takes a picture and gives me a hug. She says, "I am so proud of you."

We go home, calling my mother, brother, and sister on the way. I shower, and in two hours we are at a coworker's party. I had promised I would attend, no matter what happened. "Oh my God!" Jim, my office friend, says as he sees Linda and me approaching. "I can't believe you made it!"

Wolf Blitzer and his wife, Lynn, are standing right there.

"Why?" Wolf asks. "Where were you?"

"Well," I say, "it's kind of a long story."

TWENTY-SIX POINT TWO

our half marathons, three full marathons, one 55-mile ultramarathon, and 2,000 miles of training all in one year. From a standstill.

The day after Stone Mill, I sleep in. Linda and I enjoy a late breakfast, after which she leaves on a day trip to see her parents. I awaken Ali, and we drive to the trail.

"What are these for?" Ali asks as she spots some of the green and yellow race ribbons fluttering on a bush.

"That's how they marked the course."

"That's cool," she says.

"Some people got lost anyway."

"Even cooler."

My legs are bone-tired but not as sore as I expected, so we roam into the woods. Looking at the hills and hearing the leaves crunch, I am filled with emotion. Part of me wants to shout for joy. Part of me wants to cry. Part of me wants to get sick. Removed from the race, seeing the trail in the light of a new day, the enormity of the task is overwhelming. Closing my eyes, I feel the surging, bucking ground beneath me. I envision the lurching falls, the blinding fatigue, the seeping cold, and the feverish pain. I see the whole long, improbable, inconceivable path that led to this point.

"Was it hard?" Ali asks.

"Physically it was the hardest thing I've ever done."

"Did it hurt?"

"Oh yes."

"Did you think about stopping?"

"Many times."

"Then why did you do it?"

Her question deserves more than the pat "Because it was there" or "I wanted to show you how to take on a great challenge," so I ponder it as we walk back out of the woods.

I think about all my doubts. In no way had I been truly prepared to take on such a task. The idea of rising to a single marathon had seemed all but impossible the previous Thanksgiving. I was a middle-aged man in dubious shape. I ate all the wrong foods at odd hours. I worked too much and stayed up too late. I slept fitfully on good nights, barely at all on bad ones.

My daily schedule was so crowded that I hardly had time for haircuts. Like so many others, I worried about being pushed aside in my profession. So I responded to e-mails in the middle of the night and took calls in the wee hours of the morning. I had already surrendered many of my hobbies to the ceaseless needs of the newsroom, and yet with each year, I was stepping up my commitment to getting the job done.

Contact with my family had been as strong as it could be under the circumstances, but they knew how badly I was stressed. They heard my laughter less often and saw the strain in my smile. They saw me doing something I vowed I would never do: I stopped playing—games, jokes, and music. As a little boy, I had wondered why adults, with all their power and freedom, didn't spend more time rolling in the grass, wading through creeks, throwing rocks, and scattering leaves. And one day there I was: hustling to work, dodging raindrops, and skirting the puddles I should have stomped in.

Then this idea came along. Every ounce of reason told me that running again could be a big mistake. I did it anyway. After the first marathon, I didn't blink before charging on to the next challenge, pushing into unknown and unknowable territory guided by instinct, the whole while aware of how badly I could be hurt.

And yet none of the horrid things I had feared happened. I tested my relations, my resolve, my stamina, and my strength. But I did not lose my job or surrender my family. I did not ruin my knees or destroy my back, or faint, or fail, or pitch head-long into a chasm, or slip silently beneath the river, or clutch my chest and fade into eternity.

By the time we reach the car, I have an answer for Ali.

"As people get older, life becomes all about playing it safe. We protect our jobs and our money. We guard our houses, and we try to make the world as risk-free as we can for our kids, because that is important. But along the way, you can lose yourself. You start thinking that the great adventures are all gone and that you've reached all the limits. Your sister is already out of the house. You will be soon. And I didn't want us to become some pale shadow of the family we were, with your mom and me sitting around waiting for you to call and tell us about your adventures and never taking any risks of our own. So, when I started this, I don't know, it felt like something woke up inside me. I stopped getting through my days, and I started getting into them. I guess I ran this race because I didn't want that to end."

"Did you know all that before you began?"

"I can't say I did. I suppose I learned it on the run."

"That's beautiful, Dad," she said. "Kind of wacky. But still beautiful."

We cut down one of the big signs that had been tacked up to warn drivers to watch out for lunatics crossing the road, snag a couple of ribbons from the trees, and throw the souvenirs into the back of the car. For the first time in a year, I have no training schedule ahead of me. We drive home listening to music. I think about the song that had been an inspiration running through my head toward the end of the race, "I Can See Clearly Now" by Johnny Nash.

When we arrive home, I sit on the front porch. The afternoon is warmer than it was the day before, and I am comfortable in my jacket and jeans. The struggles of the trail seem a lifetime ago. I pull out my phone and dial. Another rings in Atlanta.

"Hey, runner, how was it?" Ronnie's voice is brimming with happiness.

"It was long," I say. "Very long."

"You have to tell me all about it . . ."

For the next hour I tell the tale of every hill and valley, every creek and crag, every sure step and teetering tumble. Our words spill over each other as we analyze the race, dissect my preparation, laugh over my mistakes, and celebrate the climactic end. We talk about the way our saga started, what race she is planning to run next, and when we might run together again.

"Did you ever imagine it would turn out like this when you asked me to help you run a marathon?" I say when the conversation slows.

There is a long pause.

"I guess I can tell you now," she says. "I never thought I'd finish."

"What?"

"I thought I'd follow the training schedule through Christmas break, go back to college, tell you my workload was too heavy, and then give up."

"If that was the plan, why did you ask me to do it?"

"Because I know it's not always easy being a dad, or working as hard as you do. I know you and Mom have given up a lot of things for Ali and me. And for you, running was one of them. When you were at my cross-country meets or we passed a road race on the way to my soccer games, I could see how much you wanted to be out there. And the only reason you weren't was that it would take time away from us. Anyway, I figured you'd never take up marathoning again for yourself, but I was pretty sure you'd do it for me."

"So why did you go through with the marathon?"

"I guess I just forgot to quit."

There is another long pause.

"There is something I still don't understand," I say. "When I kept on running, you were worried about Mom and Ali and all those hours I was out on the roads, especially near the end. Why didn't you try to convince me to ease up?"

"Because despite everything else, we could all see how much it was helping. Yeah, you were tired and you were gone a lot, but you were happier too. You were playing again. We all knew the hardest, most time-consuming training would not go on forever. And even if it seemed like you were running away a lot, we knew you were really running back to us."

"I wish you were here," I say finally. "I would give you my medal."

"I didn't run the race," she says.

"I know, but without you, I never would have started."

I am not a great athlete, and I never will be. Many runners my age, older, and younger, male and female, can outpace me any day. But since my year of running dangerously, I have completed two more ultramarathons over 50 miles each. Friends on the trail keep urging me to try a 100-miler. Maybe I will. I continue racking up traditional marathons. Ronnie has completed in a dozen half marathons, including the ones she ran in Rome and London during her studies abroad. Ali is now at Georgia Tech too, and she has expressed interest in training for a half. And Linda is signed up for a 9-miler—her longest race ever.

Nola sleeps a lot.

And yet running isn't the dominant force in our household. We like it, but primarily because it helps us enjoy our lives more than we have for years. When the girls are home during holidays and breaks between semesters, we all do a better job of putting aside our daily challenges and frustrations to enjoy our fleeting moments together. We cook great meals, tell great stories, and spend great hours in the open air no matter the season. We laugh more, hug more, and dance more.

This is the real reason I love running like an idiot against the miles, against the calendar, and against the odds. Running puts me in touch with the moment, and reminds me how each one is rare and precious. As we get older, it is easy to believe in failure, cynicism, bad intentions, and worse plans. It is hard to believe in honest effort, the kindness of strangers, and true challenges that can be honestly conquered. Running pushes all the bad aside and brings all the good my way.

I run for exultation, beauty, joy, and art.

And I run to show my daughters that life is worth more than just living. It is worth loving, deeply and passionately, in a way that looks forward and sees an endless road—inevitable and ideal.

ACKNOWLEDGMENTS

My Year of Running Dangerously is based entirely on my memories and my research, so any mistakes or omissions are mine. However, the successes must be shared with others.

Ronnie celebrated every triumph, and gently nudged me toward the finish line each time I flagged. She, first and foremost, is the reason this tale became a book. Ali consistently brought her sweetness, intelligence, and humor to my side, lifting me from the despair that haunts any long road. Linda drove me to trailheads, kept track of registration deadlines, tolerated reeking exercise clothing, and endured endless conversations about racing and writing. She was, is, and will ever be the embodiment of selflessness. Collectively, the three of them reminded me that this journey was always about more than just running. This book is theirs as much as mine.

My brother and friend Robert deserves a shout-out for teaching me about toughness and tenacity, and my sister, Chris, is the best cheerleader anyone could want. My mother, June, and my late father, Dale, taught me to love the outdoors, good stories, laughter, and life, all of which made this whole adventure not only possible but also desirable.

Janet Pawson is more than my agent. She is my longtime friend, and without her I would have been lost. David Rosenthal is more than my publisher. His praise for the original manuscript actually made me taller, and his gentle suggestions for improvement were masterly. Every writer should be so lucky. Aileen Boyle and the team at Penguin/Blue Rider are superb, and if they can get David onto the trail with me they'll be miracle workers.

My good friends and encouraging colleagues from CNN are too numerous to name, but I will note that my bureau chief, Sam Feist, Wolf Blitzer, the New Media Team, and the ever-talented Katie Ross Dominick, who was my patient producer, never so much as blinked when my escapades threatened to collide with work.

Last, I need to thank the runners who helped me along the way. My dear friend Scott Strider showed me long ago what real dedication is all about. The extraordinary Meb Keflezighi and his brother Merhawi have made me feel welcome in the company of athletic greatness. And to all the volunteers, race organizers, runners, and their families I've met on the way, thank you for filling the roads with hope and inspiration. You are the reason I like running in the middle of the pack: It makes it easier to pat you on the back for all you do.

ABOUT THE AUTHOR

When he is not running, Tom Foreman chases down news as he has for nearly forty years, including natural disasters, riots, murders, political campaigns, scandals, plane crashes, economic upheavals, criminal high jinks, sports, wildfires, droughts, and the occasional story on animal husbandry. He started working in radio during high school when he realized that his teenage magic show would never pay the rent. He has since worked for ABC News and the National Geographic Channel, and is now at CNN.

Tom loves a good road trip; he has been to all fifty states many times and more than twenty countries. He can get into difficulties in French, Spanish, and Russian but can't get out of trouble in any of those languages, as evidenced by the fact that he once nearly accidentally bought a cat in Moscow. He has pioneered the use of many of the most advanced technologies in the news business today, including 3-D virtual imaging and touchscreens.

Having grown up in an Air Force family and moved many times, Tom lays claim to several places as his home, among them South Dakota, Illinois, Alabama, and Colorado. That said, his heart belongs to Louisiana, where he and his wife, Linda, began their married life in New Orleans. Currently they live in Bethesda, Maryland, where he plays guitar and piano, paints, cooks, reads, goes to movies, and irritates the dog. He and Linda eagerly await every visit by their lovely daughters, Ronnie and Ali, and they like phone calls too—that's a hint, girls.

This is not his first book, but it is the first that amounted to anything. He wrote a novel in the 1990s that was never published, so you could argue he just practiced typing a lot. Tom found it odd to write this note in the third person. He is virtually certain that if he ever met Jimmy Kimmel they would be friends.